Endorsements

Mina and Yvon Attia are amazing people with an amazing story who have written an amazing book. Coming from the Coptic Orthodox background, it is awesome to see what the Holy Spirit is doing in Yvon and Mina's lives in regard to healing. Yvon sees me as a spiritual father to her, perhaps because of her attending the Global School of Supernatural Ministry. When I read the manuscript, I was taken by the amazing stories they share with us. The manuscript was engaging, encouraging, enlightening, and enlivening. I encourage anyone interested in learning more about healing to study not only their story but the lessons they have learned about healing. The principles they give are important, biblical, and practical. I believe you will find *Revealing the Healer* to be a major source of encouragement. Anyone interested in learning about healing should read this book.

Randy Clark, D. Min.
Overseer of the Apostolic Network of Global Awakening
Founder of Global Awakening

Yvon Attia's new book, *Revealing the Healer,* recounts her own journey into saving faith, to faith in God for healing, to becoming a healing minister. Her healing journey is entwined with her recovery from the devastation of seeing her uncle killed by Islamic terrorists to finding freedom through forgiveness, to seeing her own body healed of damage caused by an automobile accident. To know Yvon is to know her ardor and devotion to the Lord, and this pure devotion shines through the pages of her book.

In these pages, Yvon explores the scriptural basis of healing, the methods Jesus used in healing, and the role of faith. She also writes about the ever-present question of why some may not find healing when they need it. Both the novice to healing and the seasoned practitioner will find something to encourage them on the road to healing in this book. May you also find new encouragement, faith, and hope as you read it.

KEN FISH
Founder of Kingdom Fire Ministries

REVEALING THE HEALER

REVEALING THE HEALER

A COMPLETE GUIDE TO MANIFESTING THE HEALING POWER OF JESUS

YVON ATTIA

DESTINY IMAGE® PUBLISHERS, INC.

P.O. Box 310, Shippensburg, PA 17257-0310

"Promoting Inspired Lives."

This book and all other Destiny Image and Destiny Image Fiction books are available at Christian bookstores and distributors worldwide.

Cover design by Eileen Rockwell

Interior design by Terry Clifton

For more information on foreign distributors, call 717-532-3040.

Reach us on the Internet: www.destinyimage.com.

ISBN 13 TP: 978-0-7684-5392-8

ISBN 13 eBook: 978-0-7684-5393-5

ISBN 13 HC: 978-0-7684-5395-9

ISBN 13 LP: 978-0-7684-5394-2

For Worldwide Distribution.

1 2 3 4 5 6 7 8 / 24 23 22 21 20

ACKNOWLEDGMENTS

I would like to say a special thank you to every individual that helped in making this book a reality.

I would like to thank my amazing, faithful, and caring husband for his enormous love, support, and sacrifice throughout the writing of this book. When I felt the prompting of the Holy Spirit to write this book, Mina knew this was God. He encouraged me to step out and share with others what God has done in our lives. His obedience to the Holy Spirit throughout our journey, and despite many challenges, made this book possible. I want to especially thank him for giving room to the Holy Spirit to fill our lives and transform our thinking.

I would like to thank my two amazing children, Esther and Raphael, for their encouragement, sacrifice, and endurance during the writing of this book. Both Esther and Raphael endured many trials with us, yet they continued to believe in the healing ministry.

I would like to thank my family for their support and encouragement, especially my grandfather, Reverend Anis Hanna, for modeling Christ and His love since a very young age. I would like to thank my father and mother, Albert and Fawzia Hanna, who always sacrifice endless hours looking after our children during ministry time and travel.

I would like to thank my spiritual father Apostle Guillermo Maldonado for all his support and love. He has been a huge blessing to me and has impacted my ministry and life beyond measure. His life and dedication in bringing the supernatural is relentless and selfless. I will always be grateful for how God used him in my life.

I would like to thank Samuel Estefanos, the founder and director of the Middle East's largest Arabic Christian channel, AlKarma TV. He has supported us throughout our journey and made it possible for us to broadcast Arabic and English programs about divine healing. We have seen God's healing hands throughout these programs, which in turn encouraged us to write the book *Revealing the Healer*.

I would like to thank Dr. Randy Clark for endorsing the book. Dr. Randy's journey, life, and ministry has impacted us in a major way. His teaching and passion have revolutionized our hearts and minds. I am forever thankful for the impartation he has deposited into us.

I would like to thank Ken Fish for writing the foreword to the book. Ken has been a huge support to us throughout our journey. His dedication and teaching impacted us in a huge way. His prayers and support encouraged us during difficult times and made us push forward.

I would like to thank our ministry team for their love and support. We embarked on this journey together, and much of what we have learned was made possible because of their trust and endurance.

CONTENTS

FOREWORD

Yvon Attia's new book, *Revealing the Healer,* recounts her own journey into saving faith, to faith in God for healing, to becoming a healing minister. Her healing journey is entwined with her recovery from the devastation of seeing her uncle killed by Islamic terrorists to finding freedom through forgiveness, to seeing her own body healed of damage caused by an automobile accident. To know Yvon is to know her ardor and devotion to the Lord, and this pure devotion shines through the pages of her book.

In these pages, Yvon explores the scriptural basis of healing, the methods Jesus used in healing, and the role of faith. She also writes about the ever-present question of why some may not find healing when they need it. Both the novice to healing and the seasoned practitioner will find something to encourage them on the road to healing in this book. May you also find new encouragement, faith, and hope as you read it.

KEN FISH
Founder, Kingdom Fire Ministries

INTRODUCTION

R eading the New Testament can be very overwhelming and very challenging. We can't read the Gospels without taking notice of Jesus' healing ministry. Jesus was and still is a master healer; He healed whosoever, from whatsoever. Jesus moved out of great compassion and revealed the Father's heart. Through His ministry, the lepers were cleansed, the mute spoke, the deaf heard, the lame walked, and the dead were raised. Jesus demonstrated great authority over demons and destroyed the works of the devil. As a result, multitudes were healed and believed in Him.

The difficulty began when I read that portion of the Bible where Jesus promises that those who believe would do more than He did. This was my biggest challenge as I continued to read the Gospels. I grew up in church, being a Christian all my life, and I'd never witnessed one healing. I was taught that Jesus healed because He is God in flesh and was trying to prove His divinity. Doing more works than Jesus meant reaching more people in evangelism through television and media but had nothing to do with doing what Jesus did. I believed in the supernatural sovereign intervention of God healing people. But I was in a dilemma. Because Jesus gave His followers power and authority to destroy the works of the devil, while the church was focused only on evangelism.

This frustration started growing inside of me, and I started to ask God many questions. I started to feel that these questions were affecting my faith and allowing doubt to come in. As a result, I brushed off the frustration and tried not to think about it, despite God healing me after falling from a three-story building. Everything changed for me when I experienced the baptism of the Holy Spirit. My relationship with the Lord skyrocketed, and this was the start of God healing me from a skin condition. I thought God sovereignly healed me. I didn't know that He was answering my prayers, was giving solutions to my dilemmas, and was about to train me to see every healing miracle in the Bible take place in front of my own eyes.

As a result, I decided to write this book—first, to testify to the faithfulness of God through what He has done in my life. In this book, I share my personal testimony to encourage the Body of Christ to step out and take risks.

My simple message is that if God is able to use me, He can use anybody. He uses willing, ordinary people to perform super and extraordinary things for His glory. It is time to believe that we are equipped, called, anointed, and appointed.

The second primary reason for writing this book is to share biblical truths about divine healing, which I have learned on my journey so far. Jesus said you will know the truth and the truth shall set you free (John 8:32). This book contains biblical truths about the nature of God as the God who heals. Healing is God's nature, it is who He is, it is one of His attributes. As the Book of Exodus rightly put it, He is Jehovah Rapha, the God who heals (Exodus 15:26).

The book explains foundational biblical teaching about divine healing and truths such as God's willingness to heal at all times, and that healing was already obtained for us by the cross of Christ. The book exposes many lies that hinder many people from receiving their healing. Lies such as God inflicting sickness to teach them something, or not being worthy to receive healing, or the condition of having great faith to receive healing.

The book will answer many important questions that seem to occupy people's minds—questions such as, "Why do some people get healed while others do not?" More importantly, the book will equip believers to heal the sick in Jesus' name. Different keys to heal the sick are also discussed.

Secret keys in the healing ministry, such as intimacy and trust, are discussed in depth, while powerful testimonies are mentioned to build faith and restore hope. More importantly, I wrote about our journey in the ministry so far, how we started the ministry, and mentioned some of the difficulties we have faced in the journey so far, just to encourage others to keep going and press on, for He who called us is faithful.

My heart is to encourage those who need healing and to remind them that our God still heals today. He is the same yesterday, today, and forever (Hebrews 13:8). I am also believing that this book will encourage, release, and equip believers to step out and heal the sick, raise the dead, cure those with leprosy, and cast out demons (Matthew 10:1). By doing that as believers, we would share and experience the apostle Paul's excitement when he testified that God had done everything through him to bring the Gentiles to faith. He said, "They were convinced by the power of miraculous signs and wonders and by the power of God's Spirit. In this way, I have fully presented the Good News of Christ from Jerusalem all the way to Illyricum" (Romans 15:19 NLT).

My heart is to minister as Jesus did and teach others to do the same. Our Lord proclaimed the Kingdom through teaching the Kingdom's message, and He demonstrated the Kingdom through healing the sick and casting out demons. He later said that the harvest is plentiful, but the workers are few. He said to His disciples to pray for the Lord of the harvest to send more workers into His fields (Matthew 9:38). You are an answer to Jesus' prayer, and God's desire is to work through you because you have been united to Christ. The battle has been won, and Christ disarmed the spiritual rulers and authorities by His victory over the cross (Colossians 2:15). It is time for the Bride of Christ to rise and realize that through Christ we have full authority and power. In Him, we are called to destroy the work of the enemy and bring heaven to earth.

I pray that this book shall be a blessing, and that healing will be released in your body as you read it in Jesus' name. We take authority over all sickness and demons in Jesus' name. I command all sickness to leave your body. I speak wholeness and healing over you in Jesus' name. I pray total restoration over every organ, and I rebuke every disease in Jesus' name.

Chapter 1

MY INITIAL MIRACULOUS HEALING

My journey with God's miraculous healing began at a very young age. I was six at the time and was living with my family in Cairo, Egypt. We were living in a humble apartment located on the third floor. The building was quite old, and oftentimes we were out of water supply due to failure in the water pump system. One night, when the water supply was out, my mother left me with my younger brother at home and went to get water. It was about six in the evening, and for some reason Mum took longer than expected. I started to get anxious and decided to go out to the balcony to look for her. I opened the balcony door, grabbed a high chair, and climbed on it. I was looking out for Mum, and as I was looking I fell from the three-story building. As I was falling, I saw light beings surround me; they looked like angels to me. I tried to hold on to the clotheslines of the second floor, but they tore, and I landed on the ground level, straight on my back.

I was in so much pain and felt paralyzed. I remember being surrounded by so many people and could hear their loud voices in my ears. Some were in great shock and were crying; others were trying to get me to speak, to see if I was still conscious. In the middle of the crowd, I could hear my mum screaming very loudly as she was informed that the young girl who had fallen from the building was actually her daughter.

Later, my father arrived on the scene. He was in great shock and was crying hysterically. Not long after, the ambulance arrived, and I was transferred on a stretcher to the emergency ward of the hospital. The emergency crew did all they could to get me to the nearest emergency ward. They were unsure if I would actually make it. I will never forget looking at my father's face and watching his tears roll down as he kept saying, *"My dream was to see you grow up, to see your family, and your children. I never thought this day would come."*

After arriving in the emergency ward, I was diagnosed with a fracture in the spine, broken right leg, and a possibility of brain hemorrhage. The doctors informed my parents that I might not make it through the night, and if I did survive I would definitely be wheelchair bound. As the clock ticked and the night moved on, family and friends were praying for my healing. As they were praying, I gradually became conscious of everything around me. The members of medical staff were shocked as they watched me improve. Medical checkups revealed no hemorrhage in the brain! While the family was thankful for a positive report, they kept praying and believing in God that I would not be wheelchair bound and that God would completely heal me.

God healed me completely, and I miraculously recovered. The doctors knew this was the hand of God and declared that this was no less than a major miracle.

Although I didn't witness many healings growing up, this experience made me certain that God still heals. But the way I understood this was that these healing miracles are not the norm and do not happen very often.

The following year, our family faced a very difficult and challenging time as Islamic terrorists murdered many faithful believers due to their faith in Christ. One of these faithful believers was my dear uncle who was married to my aunty and left two innocent children. His crime was that he had tattooed a cross on his wrist. Seeing him dead, with blood gushing from his body, left me broken, hurt, and full of fear. My father knew that we were under serious persecution due to our faith. He knew that living in Egypt was becoming impossible and very dangerous. As a result, he insisted that we needed to migrate to Australia.

In 1988, God miraculously opened a door for us and we migrated to Australia. Leaving Egypt felt like leaving slavery, leaving Islam, leaving pain and hurt, and getting ready for a brand-new start. However, my experiences formed a different view of God than that of others. I formed the view that because God is sovereign, He is responsible for everything that has happened. In other words, God could have stopped the killing, but He didn't. This meant that He allowed it, and that I am meant to be thankful for the good and the bad. At that time, my faith was not mature enough to understand that God is a good Father and that we have an enemy whose plan is to kill, steal, and destroy (John 10:10).

I also formed a view that all Muslims were evil and should be avoided at all costs. Once again, I wasn't mature enough to distinguish between Muslims and Islam. I didn't understand that Muslims are victims of Islam, and that we should love them unconditionally and lead them to Christ. I also formed a negative view of myself. I saw myself as weak, limited, and helpless. Little did I know that I am the righteousness of God in Christ (2 Corinthians 5:21), formed in His image (Genesis 1:27), and loved by Him (John 15:9-17).

MY CONVERSION EXPERIENCE

Four years after my arrival in Australia, I started to become a rebellious teenager who didn't want much to do with God. I wanted to fit into the Australian culture and wanted freedom, as I perceived it. My relationship with God was cold and ordinary. I would usually say a quick prayer before bed and occasionally read the Bible. One day, a friend invited me to a youth group, and I agreed to go. As I sat to listen, the topic of the night was "Real Freedom." The speaker mentioned John 8:34: *"I tell you the truth, everyone who sins is a slave of sin"* (NLT). I realized that day that I might have left Egypt, the land of slavery, but Egypt was yet to leave me. I realized that I had misunderstood freedom altogether. Freedom is not about doing what you want, when you want. It is about being set free from the power of sin and living for righteousness.

That night, I made a decision that changed the course of my entire life. I surrendered the ownership of my life to the lordship of Jesus. That night, I declared that I had died with Christ and that the power of sin over my life was broken (Romans 6:7). This declaration was so powerful to the level that I felt that my old way of thinking and my old inner desires had come to an end. Great love flooded my heart for Jesus, and I knew on the inside that I was a child of God, created in Christ Jesus for good works (Ephesians 2:10).

MY HOLY SPIRIT ENCOUNTER

Life went on, and soon I got married to my amazing, loving husband, Mina. We met at his Coptic Orthodox church. Despite our differences in the way we understood God, we fell in love and soon got married. God blessed us with two amazing children, Esther and Raphael. We established a chain of pharmacies and got heavily involved in business life. We traveled extensively and desired to grow the pharmacy chain. We attended the church each Sunday and I helped out in Sunday school.

Soon after, I began to feel a sense of emptiness in my life. Everything seemed meaningless. Something was missing, despite all the vacations and the building of a brand-new house. Theological disputes started to increase between me and my husband. I knew he loved Jesus, but I wasn't sure if he was born again. I started to view my husband as religious. Mina was the leader of the deacons in the church and was in line to become an ordained orthodox priest. He wanted us to attend only the Orthodox church and listen to Orthodox sermons. Nothing else was ever allowed in our home. As the years went by, I began to get tired of these traditional views and became desperate to see my husband encounter Jesus in a real way. I promised God that I would never break up my family due to denominational differences. But I was seeking freedom and really desired for my husband to encounter Jesus in a real way. My husband's understanding of being born again was different from mine. According to the Orthodox church, one is born again when baptized as a baby and anointed with oil. However, according to my biblical understanding at the time, one is born again when one has a personal encounter with Jesus.

These theological disputes continued to increase. I always wanted to prove that I was right and that he was wrong. Although I had the right intentions, I went about it totally the wrong way. As the years went by, I felt that we were slowly growing apart from each other. I would pray for him daily, asking God to help get him saved. But it seemed to me the more I prayed, the more things just got worse. One day I was listening to a sermon by Joyce Myer, and she said, "If you have been praying for your husband and things are getting worse, know that God is working." I heard this, and peace filled my heart, as I knew that God was at work. I chose to surrender my problems to the Lord and trust Him with the results. During this time, we had moved houses and we moved to a different Orthodox church.

At the new church, I met this lady who seemed very different from most people I had met at the old church. She seemed to be on fire for God. She also felt the hunger inside my heart for the Lord. I told her that my dream and the desire of my heart was to see my husband encounter

Christ in a real way. She told me words that I couldn't really understand. She said, "Let's focus on Yvon first."

I asked her, "What do you mean?"

She looked at me and replied, "You need to be filled with the Holy Spirit!"

I was furious and said to her, "I am filled with the Holy Spirit." I even quoted Scripture to convince her:

> *So I want you to know that no one speaking by the Spirit of God will curse Jesus, and no one can say Jesus is Lord, except by the Holy Spirit* (1 Corinthians 12:3 NLT).

She simply replied, "Let's try to catch up and I will explain it all to you." I agreed, and we set a date.

The following day, I wasn't able to drive to work. I was in tears, and with tears in my eyes I asked God, "If there was such a thing as being filled with the Holy Spirit, why am I not experiencing it?" At the time I was thirty-three years old and was desperate for God. I decided to visit the local Christian bookstore and found a book about being filled with the Spirit. The book explained so much to me, and I knew that being filled with the Spirit is essential for witnessing, intimacy, receiving the gifts of the Spirit, and having the fruit of the Spirit. The more I read, the more I became desperate for the Lord to fill me. Everything in me desired more of God, at whatever cost.

At that time, I was going into week three and loving the book. The book was almost coming to an end and I still hadn't received anything. The book was explaining the following passage:

> *On the last day, the climax of the festival, Jesus stood and shouted to the crowds, "Anyone who is thirsty may come to me! Anyone who believes in me may come and drink! For the Scriptures declare, 'Rivers of living water will flow from his heart.'"* (When he said "living water," he was speaking of the Spirit, who would be given to everyone believing in him. But the Spirit had not yet been given, because Jesus had not yet entered into his glory) (John 7:37-39 NLT).

I imagined myself as one of those people on the last day of the festival. After following all the rituals and laws of the festival, I was still hungry and thirsty for more. As Jesus raised His voice to call out for thirsty people, I knew He was calling me. He was calling me to come to Him, not to religious customs and rituals, but to Him, to drink from Him so that rivers of living water would flow out of my innermost part to quench my thirst.

That day, something supernatural took place. I was alone in the car and all the windows were locked. I found myself repeating John 7:37. My tongue was locked on this verse. All I can remember is just repeating it over and over again. Suddenly I found myself overwhelmed with unspeakable joy and peace. I found myself speaking a very strange language, which I wasn't able to understand. Yet it was like a fountain gushing out of my belly. I felt heat come into my head and run through my entire body. The experience was overwhelming. I knew that I was being baptized in the Holy Spirit with the evidence of speaking in tongues. I loved my new prayer language and couldn't wait to be alone so that I could pray with it. It seemed like I found a treasure, a hidden world of joy. Things started making so much more sense to me. Jesus said to the Samaritan woman, *"God is a spirit"* (John 4:24 TPT), and therefore I needed to connect with Him at the level of the spirit.

For the first time, I enjoyed prayer and felt that my spirit was being built. I learned so much about my new best friend, "Holy Spirit." I learned that the Holy Spirit is a person equal to the Father and Jesus, that He is the promise of the Father to the Church. His role is to reveal the love of the Father, to comfort, to empower, to witness, and to perform signs and wonders. I learned to greet Him in the morning and acknowledge Him in everything I do. As I prayed, I would feel power enter my body and unexplainable joy flood my mind. My passion for the Word of God grew and I started to witness to anyone. The first miracle took place one month later, when my husband miraculously surrendered his heart to the Lord and got filled with the Holy Spirit. What was unachievable in thirteen years was achieved after one month of being filled with the power of the Holy Spirit!

Chapter 2

BEING CALLED INTO THE HEALING MINISTRY

MY PERSONAL HEALING

Getting into the healing ministry was a gradual journey of discovery and adventure. I had learned so much about the Holy Spirit, and one of the verses that really spoke to my heart was John 16:13, which says that the Holy Spirit is the Spirit of truth who guides us into all truth. I was constantly asking the Holy Spirit to teach me and guide me into all truth. I learned to be still in His presence, to wait on Him, and learn from Him. I loved His presence and was happy and content to just enjoy and host His presence.

I had been suffering from a skin virus (warts) for three years before my experience with the Holy Spirit. Having pharmacies of our own, I had tried every single product on the market, but all was to no avail. My condition was getting worse and I was running out of options. This virus was affecting my self-esteem and it eventually forced me to cover my olive skin every time. It was causing pain, shame, itchiness, and discomfort. I visited my local doctor, who tried to burn off the warts with liquid nitrogen. This process was extremely painful, and soon after these warts would start to grow once again. My local doctor referred me to an expensive dermatologist, who, after seeing me, offered no hope of cure. He told me that the roots of those warts were quite deep, and the only temporary treatment was to continue burning them off.

Although I was filled with the Holy Spirit and was constantly praying in the Spirit, I never asked God to heal me. I understood God to be more concerned with spiritual issues like getting souls saved, but not about material things such as healing my body. I had no idea that God really cared about my body and paid the full price of my physical healing when He was physically crucified on the cross. Christ was crucified as a whole man (spirit, soul, and body), to redeem not only souls, but also the entire man (save their spirit, deliver their soul, and heal their body).

That day, as I walked out of the dermatologist's room, I was filled with feelings of hopelessness. I didn't know what to do next. I thought to myself, "What a shame I have to live this way." As I was sitting quietly in my car, thinking deeply about these issues, I heard the quiet whisper of the Holy Spirit telling me, *"Did you know I still heal today?"*

I found myself responding, "Yes, Lord, I know You still heal."

Then I heard the gentle whisper say, *"Then why don't you ask Me to heal you?"*

I found myself responding, "Lord, what if I ask, and I don't get healed? That will shake my relationship with You and bring doubt in." I found myself saying, "Lord, I love our relationship and I don't want to shake it in any way or manner."

Then I heard Him say to me, *"Look at your skin, and take photos, because seven days from today, you will be completely healed."*

Hearing this made me very scared. I thought, "Was that God or was that me speaking? Am I going crazy and losing my mind?" Suddenly, I thought to myself, "What am I going to lose? Absolutely nothing." I grabbed my phone and took pictures of my deformed skin. I kept quiet the whole time until I became certain that this was really God and that He was going to heal me. Looking at my skin seemed impossible, especially in seven days. But

I was reminded of the verse that literally says, *"What is impossible with man is possible with God"* (Luke 18:27).

As days passed by, I was examining my skin, trying to notice any difference. I could see that gradually the warts started to get very dry and hard. They were no longer painful and wet. On the seventh day, I literally flicked them all off. One by one, they fell off. My faith leaped and I felt that the love and compassion of God were practical. It was more than words written on a page. I fell in love with God even more and was so thankful for His healing hands. However, at the time I still believed that this was not the norm and that God had performed a supernatural act to strengthen me.

Seeing God Heal Others

After this encounter, I kept pressing into God and continued to ask the Holy Spirit for more of Him. Both my husband and I were invited to a pastors' and leaders' conference in Malaysia. We had newly joined the local church and didn't really understand why we were invited. In faith, we went, seeking God and asking the Holy Spirit to show us. When we asked if we could leave our two children with my mother, she explained to me that the week of our travel was the same week of her operation. She had been on the waiting list for two long years to do a shoulder replacement. She had damaged her shoulder and was in severe pain. My father had been assisting her for the last two years.

Hearing this, I was very disappointed, first because I didn't want my mother to miss out on her operation, and second because I really wanted to attend the conference. She had received a letter from the hospital informing her of the dates and explaining that these dates were not open to change. I took the letter and prayed. In my supplication, I said, "Lord, I am going to call the hospital and ask to postpone the date of this operation to the following week. If it is Your will for us to go, let the hospital agree, and if it is not Your will, let them refuse to change the dates." After prayer, I called the hospital, and to my great surprise the office assistant agreed to change the dates with no problem. I was so happy and knew that God was planning a great surprise.

When we landed, we were called in and asked to translate the conference sessions into Arabic for some overseas pastor from Egypt. While that was exciting and we felt we were serving somehow, we knew that there was more. The last night of the conference was listed as a healing service. I didn't think much of it and didn't expect anything to happen. To my surprise, a large Muslim family of about thirty people arrived, carrying a sick family member on a stretcher. This young man had been involved in a severe motorbike accident and was not recovering in hospital. The family had decided to take the risk and bring him for prayer. The person leading the service asked us all to stretch our hands toward this man and pray for his healing. He said, "Pray for him as if this man was your father or your brother."

Everyone was praying fervently as we watched. We had never in our lives witnessed anything like this. After prayer, nothing much happened, but to my surprise the pastor leading the prayer session walked up to the man on the stretcher and repeated what Peter and John said to the lame man in Acts 3:6: "Silver or gold I do not have, but what I do have I give you. In the name of Jesus Christ of Nazareth, walk." The pastor took the young man by the hands and supported him to stand. For the first time, the man stood and started walking. He was totally healed by Jesus. Straight after this incident, the pastor gave the people an opportunity to surrender their lives to the lordship of Jesus Christ. To my great shock, all the members of the Muslim family who had come in with the man on the stretcher gave their lives to Christ.

I was so excited and felt the Book of Acts had finally come to life. The Muslim family saw the healing, and that was enough for them to be saved. We didn't need to convince them or argue with them or even try and prove their religion was wrong. The healing was enough to prove to them that the Name of Jesus is above every other name. I was so excited and felt that God had revealed to me a great door for evangelism. On the other side, fear crept in, and I thought to myself, "But what if this was a demonic power? Maybe this is not God to start with, as I have never seen anything like this in my church before."

At the time, I didn't know that sickness is from the enemy and that the reason the Son of Man appeared was to destroy the works of the devil (1 John 3:8). The way Jesus destroyed the work of the devil was by healing the sick (Acts 10:38). In addition to that, if this was a demonic power, then satan would be dividing his own kingdom (Matthew 12:25). As I was thinking about what had just happened, I started praying and found myself saying, "Dear Lord, give me a sign to believe this power was from You by healing my mother. I want to go home and find her healed." I kept saying, "Lord, if that happens, then I promise You that I will dedicate my life to the healing ministry and be willing to tell the world that You still heal."

I didn't tell my husband what my prayer was about. Nevertheless, my husband prayed a similar prayer to mine without telling me. He said, "Lord, if this is You, please give me a sign and heal my father from pancreatic cancer." We both didn't communicate our prayer request to each other, yet we prayed the same type of prayer.

We arrived home, and I didn't even have the faith to tell my mother anything. I simply asked her, "Mum, what time is your operation on Monday?"

Her reply shocked me. She answered, "God performed a miracle and totally healed me."

I asked further, "When?" She mentioned the exact time I had been praying for her. She started to move her shoulder and cry. I was in tears and just knelt on the ground. I started to praise our Healer and tell Him that I would serve Him for the rest of my life. My husband had a similar experience with his father. We encouraged him to get tests done, and to our shock he was healed. Our world changed after that. Our eyes were opened, not only to the fact that God saves but also that God heals.

RECEIVING AN IMPARTATION

Up until then, I was certain that healing hadn't ceased, as some may think, and that God sovereignly heals. However, it never crossed my mind that God wanted to use me to heal. After this encounter of seeing my mother and father-in-law healed, I became hungrier for God. It seemed to me that the more God worked in my life, the hungrier I became. The more He revealed, the thirstier I was. I was willing to travel to the ends of the world to get a touch of His presence. The hunger and thirst led me to look out for Spirit-filled conferences. All I wanted was more of His presence and His love. I wanted to see more real healings and miracles. As I searched the Internet, I came across what was called "Fire Conference." I had no idea who was running the conference and what it was really about. I felt compelled to just go.

As a result, I booked tickets, organized accommodation, left my two children with my mother and drove with my husband to the conference place. The venue was about two hours from where we lived. By the time we arrived, it was dark, and it started pouring rain. However, the building was shut and empty. I became very upset and asked the restaurant next door. No one seemed to know what was going on. I sat in the car and was about to cry. I started praying. "Lord, what happened to the conference I booked?"

My husband wasn't very happy either. He said, "Maybe you missed the dates or the location." I didn't know what to do. My husband saw how upset I was and checked the website once again. Finally, he could see that due to increased attendance, they had moved the conference to a different venue. I was so relieved, as we had been getting very close to driving back home. I knew that this was spiritual warfare and that the enemy wanted to stop us from receiving something so powerful.

Eventually, we arrived at the venue, and the reception lady looked up our names and handed us our badges, along with a work booklet. Reading the heading of the booklet brought tears to my eyes. This wasn't an ordinary conference as I had thought. The booklet read, "A school of healing and impartation." God reminded me of the promise I had made earlier when I promised Him that if He would heal my mother I would dedicate my life to the healing ministry. Although I had forgotten my promise, God hadn't, and He had led me to a place where I would learn and receive an impartation.

The school was Global Awakening by Dr. Randy Clark. The teaching was amazing and powerful. I learned so much about the character of God as "the God who heals" (Exodus 15:26), the scope of healing (Psalm 103:3), the biblical basis for healing, and the provision of healing in the atonement (Isaiah 53:4). We learned how to receive words of knowledge for healing and how to pray for the sick. But most importantly, we learned that believers are commissioned and qualified to lay their hands on the sick and get them healed in Jesus' Name (Mark 16:17). We learned that Jesus commissioned the twelve disciples to heal the sick (Matthew 10:1), the sev-enty-two apostles to heal the sick, and all believers (Mark 16:17). This meant that the only qualification needed was to believe. This revelation shook my world again and set me free. I came from the Coptic Orthodox church, where we were taught that during the days of Christ the apostles healed because Christ gave them this authority, and saints healed because they were holy. Because we were not apostles or saints, according to this church, we didn't carry this authority for healing.

After days of learning and soaking up every word, Dr. Randy Clark called us to the front. He laid his hands on us to receive an impartation. As he started to pray, we felt fire consuming us. Tears were rolling down our faces as we heard him say that God would be using us to preach and teach the supernatural Gospel in the Middle East and Central Asia. He said, "You will lay your hands on the sick and they will recover." He said, "You will also become an apologist to defend the supernatural and build bridges between the Body of Christ and the supernatural."

Chapter 3

HEALING IN THE GOSPELS AND THE BOOK OF ACTS

After receiving this impartation from Dr. Randy Clark, we were both excited and puzzled. We were very excited to realize that God still heals today and that He wants to use us to heal the sick. However, we were puzzled because we didn't know where or how to start.

I knew this was a great door to evangelism. So many people are looking for proof that God is real and that He really cares and has compassion for His people. I knew that many believed and followed Jesus because they saw Him heal the sick.

*And a great crowd of people followed him because
they saw the signs he had performed by healing the
sick* (John 6:2).

To get started, we decided to enroll in the online
Christian healing certification program by Global
Awakening. One of our assessments was to read the four
Gospels and the Book of Acts and highlight all the pas-
sages that refer to healing the sick. To our surprise, most
of the four Gospels and the Book of Acts were high-
lighted. We knew that healing the sick played a major
part both in the ministry of Jesus and the early Church.
Jesus knew that sickness is the work of the devil and that
healing the sick destroys the devil's work (1 John 3:8).
As a result, Jesus traveled throughout Galilee, teaching,
preaching, and healing all kinds of disease and illness
(Matthew 4:23).

That was the same explanation Peter used when he
described the ministry of Jesus to Cornelius, who was
a Roman army officer. Peter explained to him that God
anointed Jesus of Nazareth with the Holy Spirit and with
power. As a result, Jesus went around doing good and
healing all who were oppressed by the devil, for God was
with him (Acts 10:38). We get to see how Jesus saw sickness. To Him, sickness was not a punishment from God
but, rather, oppression from the devil. And the evidence
that "God was with Him" resulted in healing "all who
were oppressed."

As a result, Jesus healed everyone who came to Him (Matthew 4:23; 8:16). The physician Luke puts it this way: *"As the sun went down that evening, people throughout the village brought sick family members to Jesus. No matter what their diseases were, the touch of his hand healed every one"* (Luke 4:40). These healings increased to the level that He was healing on the Sabbath, which is a day of complete rest and the most sacred institution among the Jews.

This has much to do with the way Jesus viewed His mission and viewed sickness. In Luke 4:18, after Jesus returned from Galilee, filled with the Holy Spirit's power, He was given the scroll of Isaiah to read. He unfolded the scroll and read the following passage:

> *The Spirit of the Lord is upon me, for he has anointed me to bring Good News to the poor. He has sent me to proclaim that captives will be released, that the blind will see, that the oppressed will be set free* (Luke 4:18 NLT).

After reading this passage, He began to speak to the people in the temple and made a shocking statement, which made the religious leaders furious and ready to kill Him. He said to them, *"The Scripture you've just heard has been fulfilled this very day!"* (Luke 4:21 NLT). In other words, "I am the expected Messiah, and my mission is to release the captives, heal the sick, and set the oppressed free."

This mission had been made clear when John the Baptist was in prison and heard about all the things Jesus was doing. John the Baptist knew that the coming Messiah would bring healing by opening the eyes of the blind, unplugging the ears of the deaf, and healing the lame (Isaiah 35:5-6). John wanted first-hand confirmation that Jesus was the expected one. Jesus didn't reply by saying yes or no. He simply stated:

> *Jesus replied, "Go back and report to John what you hear and see: The blind receive sight, the lame walk, those who have leprosy are cleansed, the deaf hear, the dead are raised, and the good news is proclaimed to the poor. Blessed is anyone who does not stumble on account of me"* (Matthew 11:4-6).

He simply stated His mission by healing the sick, even when they didn't ask. The healing of the woman who had been bent double for eighteen years reveals that she didn't expect or even ask to get healed (Luke 13:10). Luke the physician clearly tells us that the root cause of her illness was the presence of an evil spirit. Jesus immediately approached her and healed her without any hesitation. Unlike others who brought their lame, crippled, mute friends and family and laid them at His feet, this woman didn't ask for anything, yet Jesus simply healed her. When the religious leaders became indignant that Jesus healed on the Sabbath, Jesus replied:

You hypocrites! Each of you works on the Sabbath day! Don't you untie your ox or your donkey from its stall on the Sabbath and lead it out for water? This dear woman, a daughter of Abraham, has been held in bondage by Satan for eighteen years. Isn't it right that she be released, even on the Sabbath? (Luke 13:15-16)

His words reveal that sickness is likened to tying or binding someone who desperately needs water, and healing is likened to releasing or freeing someone to quench their thirst. In particular, "this dear woman" was not just anyone. She was "a daughter of Abraham." In other words, she is a descendant of Abraham and is included in the Abrahamic covenant. Blessings and healing belong to her; they are her inheritance because of who she is and not because of what she is doing. She is a daughter of Abraham and in a covenant relationship with God.

A covenant is a legally binding agreement between two parties. There are two basic types of covenants—conditional and unconditional. A conditional covenant is an agreement that is binding, where both parties must fulfill certain conditions. If either party fails, the covenant is broken. However, the Abrahamic covenant is an unconditional covenant between God and Abraham (and his descendants), where one party has to do something, while nothing is required from the other party. God made promises of blessings to Abraham that did not require any action of him (Genesis 15:18-21). God asked Abraham to bring different animals, kill them, and cut them in half. Abraham cut the animals in the middle and laid the halves side by side. Normally, in a conditional covenant, both parties walk through the halves of animals to declare that if any party breaks the covenant, it will be done to them as it has been done to those animals. However, in this grand Abrahamic covenant, God alone (carrying the smoking furnace and flaming torch) moved through the halves of the covenant, not Abraham. In fact, God caused a sleep to fall upon Abraham so that he would not be able to pass between the two halves of the animals.

Through this action, God promised that if He was to ever break the covenant, it will be done to Him as it was done to these animals. In other words, God would never break this covenant and bound Himself to it. God promised to bless Abraham and his descendants without requiring them to do anything. Abraham's only response was to believe God, as the Scripture mentions, and God counted him as righteous because of his faith (Genesis 15:6).

With this understanding in mind, Jesus sees this bent-double woman who isn't aware of her rights and, thus, never asks for her healing. All the odds are against Him. It is the Sabbath, and the religious leaders are indignant about Him. Yet He knows that this woman is "a daughter of Abraham" and that she qualifies for God's blessings. It is her right to be healed, to be free, and to be well. She is not required to achieve anything. She is simply required to receive what rightfully belongs to her.

The same promises of blessing belong to us. We need to realize that because we belong to Christ, we are Abraham's children by faith, and God's promises of blessings to Abraham belong to us (Galatians 3:29). We are included in the Abrahamic covenant through faith in Christ. We are not required to achieve anything; rather, we need to believe and receive like our father Abraham, who, against all hope, continued to believe God's promise of bearing a child. Although he was about one hundred years old and Sarah's womb was dead, yet he continued to believe that God is faithful to fulfill what He promised (Romans 4:18-22).

Even throughout the entire Book of Acts, we get to see that when healings took place, people praised God, and many were added to the Church. The first example of this is found in Acts 3, after Peter and John healed the man who had been lame for more than forty years. People were praising the Lord, and the number of believers totaled 5,000 people (Acts 4:4).

This miracle caused the disciples to be persecuted, and they were warned not to ever speak or teach in the name of Jesus (Acts 4:18). As a result of these commands, the disciples decided to get together and pray. This prayer sets the theme for the entire Book of Acts and points us to what the early Church prayed for.

> *"Now, Lord, consider their threats and enable your servants to speak your word with great boldness. Stretch out your hand to heal and perform signs and wonders through the name of your holy servant Jesus." After they prayed, the place where they were meeting was shaken. And they were all filled with the Holy Spirit and spoke the word of God boldly* (Acts 4:29-31).

As a result of this prayer, more and more people believed in the Lord; sick people were brought out onto the street on beds and mats so that Peter's shadow might fall on them and heal them (Acts 5:15). Crowds gathered from villages, bringing their sick and those possessed by evil spirits, and they were all healed.

As a result of Acts 4:29, the number of believers increased. Seven men were chosen to care for the poor. These men were not apostles nor from Jesus' disciples, yet they were full of the Holy Spirit and wisdom (Acts 6:3). Stephen, who was full of God's grace and power, performed astounding miracles and signs (Acts 6:8); while Philip, who went to preach in Samaria, gathered large crowds because they not only heard his message but saw the miraculous signs he did (Acts 8:7). Great joy filled Samaria because evil spirits were leaving their victims, and many paralyzed and lame people were healed (Acts 8:7).

As a result of the prayer in Acts 4:29, Saul is converted to Paul. Peter visits the believers in Lydda, where he encounters a man named Aeneas who had been paralyzed and bedridden for eight years. Peter heals him by a simple statement, *"Jesus Christ heals you. Get up and roll up your mat"* (Acts 9:34). Immediately, the man is healed. This healing results in a major revival, where the whole population of Lydda and Sharon turns to the Lord (Acts 9:36). From Lydda, Peter travels to Joppa, where he finds a kind, generous believer called Tabitha (which in Greek is Dorcas), who had become ill and died. Her body was washed and ready for burial. The believers hear that Peter is close by, so they call him to come as soon as possible. When Peter arrives, they take him to the upstairs room where her body is laid. He asks all those who are weeping to leave the room. Then he kneels and prays. He then turns to the body. He says, "Get up, Tabitha." Immediately, she opens her eyes and sits up. The news spreads through the whole town, and many believe in the Lord (Acts 9:42).

Paul continued his ministry in the same trail. In fact, God gave Paul the power to perform unusual miracles because usual miracles were the ordinary and the norm. Therefore, Paul operated in a different realm where unusual miracles were taking place. Handkerchiefs that had touched his body were healing the sick and expelling demons (Acts 19:11-12). Even on his final visit to Troas, before leaving for Jerusalem, he was preaching until midnight. As it was getting late, a young man by the name of Eutychus was sitting by the window. He became drowsy, fell asleep, and fell three stories to his death. Paul went down, bent over him, and took him in his arms. He told the people, "Don't worry, he's alive," and immediately continued his preaching.

This is extremely powerful. Paul didn't cause strife or pray long prayers or raise his voice. He simply bent over him and embraced him. Paul was well aware that when he embraced him, it was no longer him embracing the other man; rather, the dead young man was embracing Jesus Himself. As Paul rightfully said, *"I have been crucified with Christ and I no longer live, but Christ lives in me"* (Galatians 2:20). It was Christ living in Paul who embraced this dead man and brought life to him.

The amazing thing is that unusual miracles were the norm. After this miracle took place, we see Paul continuing his preaching as if this is just normal (Acts 20:11). Resurrecting the dead takes no more faith than healing the sick. The same Christ who heals is the one who resurrects from the dead. Healing the sick played a major part in Paul's ministry, even though he was sentenced to death.

At one time, after fourteen nights struggling in the sea of Adria and being shipwrecked, Paul finally arrived on the island of Malta. The chief officer's father was ill with fever and dysentery. Paul went in and prayed for him, and, laying his hands on him, he healed him (Acts 28:8). All the other sick people on the island heard what had happened to the chief officer's father. As a result, they came and were healed (Acts 28:9). It is no wonder Paul writes to the Romans the following:

> *Now then, it is through my union with Jesus Christ, that I enjoy an enthusiasm and confidence in my ministry for God. And I will not be presumptuous to speak of anything except what Christ has accomplished through me. For many non-Jewish people are coming into faith's obedience by the power of the Spirit of God, which is displayed through mighty signs and amazing wonders, both in word and deed. Starting from Jerusalem I went from place to place as far as the distant Roman province of Illyricum, fully preaching the wonderful message of Christ* (Romans 15:17-19 TPT).

Paul explained clearly that he preached the Gospel in word and deed. In other words, there was a demonstration of what he was teaching. The signs and wonders confirmed his proclamation. In fact, "fully preaching the Gospel" requires the display of mighty signs and wonders through the power of the Holy Spirit. In that he boasted, because Christ did everything through him to bring the non-Jewish people to faith.

Through studying these texts, it was clear to me that what was available to Peter, John, Stephen, Philip, and Paul is also available to us. It was their union with Christ and the empowering Holy Spirit that allowed them to minister to such magnitude. This is Christ's desire and answer to His prayers—that we would be joined together as one, just as Jesus and the Father are one (John 17:21). Jesus was fully united to the Father and testified that the Father, who lives in Him, does His work through Him (John 14:10). His prayer is that we would experience such perfect unity through Jesus and that through our words and deeds the world would know that the Father sent Jesus (John 17:23). Through this perfect unity, the Father will continue to do His work through us, just like He did His work through Jesus.

Chapter 4

GETTING STARTED AND REACHING THE WORLD

LAUNCHING THE HOMEGROUP

By that time, we were totally convinced that healing the sick was not a side ministry. It was an essential part of the ministry of Jesus and must be an essential part in every ministry. We didn't know how to start or where to share our message. We thought that the easiest way to get started was to invite family members and close friends to come for dinner and hopefully we could share the word.

It was early 2011, and we invited everyone to meet on the following Friday night. We were extremely excited and for days we were praying about the message and planning the entire night. The day finally arrived, and to my surprise most of the people we had invited gave one excuse or another, apologized, and were unable to make it. I was so devastated, and hopelessness grabbed hold of me. It was easy to become offended and just give up. But I am thankful for the secret place of prayer, where I was given a boost of hope and endurance to keep going and not to give up.

Without fail, we invited everyone over to our place again the following Friday, and we promised to cook them all dinner. This time, most of them turned up, and we started to open up and share about the journey that God had made us go through. We prayed with everyone and encouraged them to invite their friends and anyone who needed prayer for healing. We also let them know that our house would be open for prayer and dinner every Friday night and that they were more than welcome to invite anyone they wished.

The following Friday, a dear family member invited a newlywed couple. This couple enjoyed a loving relationship, but just before their wedding the groom had been diagnosed with thyroid cancer, and the doctors had given him a very bad report. They heard about our humble meeting and decided to come for prayer. At the end of the meeting, we asked them to stand in the middle, as we all stood around them and prayed for them. At this stage, we had no idea that we should rebuke cancer or command it to shrivel and leave. We simply prayed fervently and watched to see if anything would happen. Nothing really happened, other than the couple felt peace and comfort. The couple didn't expect anything to change, as they came from churches where healing the sick is not the norm. The groom went to get tested, and to his shock and surprise there was no trace of thyroid cancer. They contacted us and informed us of what had happened and what the doctors had said to them. We were extremely happy and felt the move of the Holy Spirit in our midst.

GOING OUT

Word about the healing of this young man went out, and the Friday meeting was attracting more and more people. It was a big commitment on our part, but we did it with joy and gladness. More people kept coming, and more healings kept happening. God was encouraging us to keep going. Not everyone we prayed for was healed, but the more we prayed for people, the more healings we saw. Even in hard cases, where we didn't see the healings we desired to see, we kept our eyes on Jesus, the author and finisher of our faith.

As the meetings increased and more foreign people kept coming, some dear friends suggested that we should no longer have the meeting at home; rather, we should hire a community hall. We followed their wishes, and this was a step of faith. Because my husband is a pharmacist, most of our friends were either pharmacists or doctors.

We hired the community hall, set the dates, designed a logo, and printed the brochures for the meeting. We sent text messages and invited everyone who crossed our minds. We purchased music equipment and tried to put together a music band. The team practiced many times before the meeting, as we were very nervous and had no idea what to do. We had never previously organized church meetings or events, but deep inside we knew this was God and that He was in the midst of this meeting.

The day finally arrived, and to our surprise many people turned up, and the hall was almost full. There were many new faces, and excitement and fear filled the atmosphere. My husband preached his first message from First Samuel 17, about young David attacking Goliath. David knew that the God who was with him was greater than anything that was coming against him. My husband reminded the people that the presence of God that's with them is greater than anything that can come against them.

At the end of the meeting, there was an opportunity for people to surrender the ownership of their life to the lordship of the Lord Jesus Christ. Following this call, we reminded people that the name of our God is Jehovah Rapha, the God who heals (Exodus 15:26). We prayed for the sick people with no expectation. We didn't have the courage to ask people to check themselves and see if they got healed. Yet straight after the meeting, a few people felt intense heat in their body, and they noticed that they got healed. We were extremely encouraged and allowed these people an opportunity to share what had happened. More people received prayer, and we were strengthened in our faith. To us, God is not dead, He is alive, and He doesn't only save, He heals and delivers also.

One older lady testified to her healing. She said that a few days prior to our meeting, she had slipped on the kitchen floor and fallen on her back. She had been taking painkillers and trying to rest. But she was still in excruciating pain and could hardly walk. As we were praying for all the sick people, she felt intense heat, and she noticed that all the pain in her body had disappeared. She was in tears and was praising God and thanking Him.

As a result of the success of the first meeting, we decided to continue these meetings monthly. The following month, we were excited and couldn't wait to see what God could do. However, we were also stressed and nervous. I was praying, and I said, "Lord, what if we pray for people and nothing really happens?"

I heard His gentle sweet voice replying, "*I will never leave you nor forsake you.*" These words filled me with peace, and also encouraged us greatly.

Before the meeting, we were praying for boldness and clarity from the Holy Spirit. We started to pray for words of knowledge and seek the Holy Spirit's direction. The worship session started, and the presence of the

Lord filled the place. After the preaching of the word, I stood up and shared a short word from Mark 5:25-34. I retold the story of this woman who had been bleeding for twelve years. The apostle Mark tells us that she had been to many physicians and had spent all she had. According to the Jewish Torah, she was unclean, and if she touched anyone, the fellow would become defiled and unclean from her touch. Despite all the above, the reputation of Jesus' compassion preceded Him and made her touch His garment. The Bible tells us that she decided within herself that if she touched His garments, she would be healed. The apostle Mark goes on to tell us that immediately she was healed and felt power enter her body. I then asked the sick people who were present if they wanted to touch His garments like this woman did. Many put up their hands and responded to the call. By then, God had revealed many accurate words of knowledge. We called them out, and many responded to them. Most of the people were healed as the glorious presence of the Lord filled the hall. We asked many to come out and share their testimonies.

Different people gave different testimonies. It was glorious, and there was a sense of indescribable joy on everyone's faces. However, opposition started rapidly. Those people who were healed went back to their churches and started to share what had happened. Church leaders who were not open to the work of the Holy Spirit made these people doubt their healing and spread rumors that God is not interested in healing bodies. God doesn't care about bodies; rather, He is more interested in saving souls. Others who came from traditional settings also faced issues as the priests were telling them that only ancient saints who died years ago are able to heal. These people were threatened to not come again for more prayers and were told that healing doesn't happen from ordinary people. Persecution also hit from within the team, who were qualified pharmacists and doctors. Those people think in a very rational manner, and their minds had not fully been renewed. To them, God doesn't heal in this manner also. They believe that God cures and heals through medicines and doctors only. For example, if someone has cancer, then God would heal them through chemotherapy. As a result, they didn't agree with us calling words of knowledge or rebuking sickness. Others believed that sickness was the will of God for people to purify themselves and bring them closer to Him. These dear believers didn't want anything to separate them from the will of God. As a result, they refused prayer and were completely against healing the sick.

We didn't know what to do. Church leaders who were not experiencing the same revival were angry with us. Some of our team members were also against it and were advising us to stop mentioning the word *healing*. As I was praying and pouring my heart out to the Lord, I heard His sweet voice telling me, *"You have only been reading about My healing miracles but didn't take the time to read about what happened to Me after these miracles."* As a result, I decided to reread each healing miracle, paying special attention to the after effect. To my surprise, I started to notice that the religious leaders were indignant about Jesus and planned to kill Him each time they saw Him heal.

A great example of this is found in John 5 after Jesus healed the lame man near the sheep gate who had been lying there for thirty-eight years. The Pharisees tried all the harder to find a way to kill Him (John 5:18). In John 9, Jesus healed a man born blind, and as a result the man who was healed was thrown out of the synagogue and Jesus was called a sinner, demon possessed, and out of His mind (John 9:24; 10:19). Even when Jesus raised Lazarus from the dead after four days, the Bible tells us that many believed in Him when they saw what had happened, while the leading priests and Pharisees were conspiring to kill Him (John 11:47). They said that Jesus performed many miraculous signs, and if they allowed Him to keep going everyone would believe in Him (John 11:47). Meanwhile, the leading priests and the Pharisees had publicly ordered that anyone seeing Jesus must report it immediately so they could arrest Him (John 11:57).

The Lord knew my heart was broken and needed healing. He opened my eyes to what Jesus went through after His healing miracles. Many think that the healing ministry is glorious, and it sure is. When God breaks in and healing takes place, it is glorious, as healing is His presence in action. However, there is pain if people are not healed or their mind is not renewed and they spread rumors about the ministry. I started to understand what Jesus meant when He said that whoever wants to follow Him must deny himself, take up his cross, and follow Him (Matthew 16:24).

I learned to deny myself and understand that I have already died with Christ. A dead person doesn't have feelings, and if I am still hurting from people's reactions, then I haven't really died. I must carry my cross, my pain of different reactions and different negative comments, and keep going. I have a clear command to heal the sick. My role is to pray for those people; God's role is to heal.

As the Holy Spirit was encouraging me and strengthening me, the third monthly meeting was fast approaching. There was fear in my heart, but I decided that by the power of the Holy Spirit I would keep going, and nothing would ever stop me. Once again, messages, texts, and emails about the meeting went out. On the actual day of the meeting, we received one call after another from different close friends telling us why they were no longer coming to the meeting. Some said, "We don't believe God heals in this way." Others had restrictions on them from different priests, while still others said, "Salvation is the most important and not healing."

Tears rolled down my face; we were very hurt and devastated. I ran to God in prayer, and asked for His support and comfort. I remember the Holy Spirit whispered in my ears, "Jesus stopped for the one; will you?"

I remember replying to the Holy Spirit by saying, "Yes, I will." That day, I got my strength together and headed to the meeting. Many people attended for the very first time. Some came to see what was going to happen, while others decided to continue. But as usual, God turned up, and the presence of His Spirit filled the place. Many reported their healing and came out to the front to give testimonies. A religious family member who was scheduled to have a knee replacement was instantly healed by Jesus and recorded her testimony.

At the end of the meeting, a man approached us and introduced himself. We personally didn't know him, but a friend had invited him. He had enjoyed the meeting and was in awe from all the testimonies he had seen and heard. He said, "This is a move of the Holy Spirit, and the world needs to know about it." He said to us that he was connected to the Middle East's largest Christian Arabic television channel (AlKarma TV). He said that we could record a live television program and teach the entire world about the God who saves, heals, and delivers. We had absolutely no idea what he was talking about. We had never spoken on television and had no media experience. We took this into prayer and decided to meet him the following week to discuss it. He encouraged us to sit behind the cameras and just share our heart and how we understood God. We agreed to give it a try and see what happens.

We turned up and just shared about how the nature of God is constant and doesn't change. He is the God who heals (Exodus 15:26); that is who He is. Healing flows out of God. He is the one who is able to forgive all my sins and heal all my diseases (Psalm 103:3). Then we prayed and concluded the episode. They sent this pilot episode to the director of the channel, and we waited in prayer. To our great surprise, the episode was approved and we set dates to start airing this program to Australia.

The day finally arrived, and we knew this was such a big deal. As the countdown started, three, two, one, my heart almost stopped. I knew that all of Australia would be watching this, and, being a live program, anyone could just call and ask any question. However, I must testify to the goodness of God. He gave us strength and courage and boldness to share His word with great love.

As we started sharing the message, our first call was received from Germany. We were shocked because we thought only Australia would be watching—we never envisioned a call coming through from another country far away from Australia. Also, we didn't know what was going on, other than receiving calls from all around the world.

At the conclusion of the episode, we found out that the founder of the channel was praying before we started, and he heard the Holy Spirit tell him, "Open every satellite and let the whole world hear." He was obedient to the call and took on a huge challenge. But God is amazing and carried us through this journey. This weekly live program has now been four years running. I can only testify to the love and goodness of God through it. We watched God do countless miracles and saw many Muslims come to the Lord. It has been amazing, and with all the above in mind we are thankful and humbled by how the Lord is using us, and we also know that we are only scratching the surface and that the best is yet to come.

Chapter 5

BIBLICAL UNDERSTANDING OF SICKNESS AND HEALING

DIFFERENT VIEWS ON HEALING

From reading the previous chapters, one would see that healing is an essential part of biblical teaching. As we went on praying for the sick, many were responding differently to our prayers, especially when it came to praying for physical healing. Many came to ministry time with their own preconceived ideas and thoughts on the subject of healing. These ideas had been formed from a young age by their environment, culture, upbringing, and faith. These preconceived ideas and thoughts greatly influenced their healing by either opening a way for the Holy Spirit to work or completely blocking the way.

THE WESTERN MIND-SET

In the Western world, when someone is diagnosed with a physical disease or an illness, the first thing they tend to do is go to the doctor and seek medical advice. (We are not attacking doctors; in actual fact, we are praying for them.) They don't see the need to also pray for their physical problem because, in their mind, God is only concerned with spiritual conditions, not physical conditions. This position puts us in a very dangerous place, because when someone receives a bad doctor's report and God is divorced from the picture, the doctor becomes their God, and they start saying, "But the doctor said..." instead of believing God's promises and taking a firm hold of those great promises.

In the Western mind-set, there is a separation between spiritual reality and material reality. Sickness is viewed as a matter of cause and effect for doctors to resolve, while spiritual challenges are matters of faith for pastors and theologians. The Western mind-set has been greatly affected by the dualistic understanding that entered the Western church through Thomas Aquinas in the thirteenth century and affected the way we view the human body. Thomas Aquinas was an influential Catholic priest, philosopher, and theologian.

Thomas embraced several ideas put forward by Aristotle (384-322 B.C.), who argued that human beings are categorized as having the spiritual capacity, a soul (the psyche—the mind, emotions, and will), and living in a body (bodily organs). We are seen as different parts rattling around under the skin. We are fixed by changing bad parts. Thomas called Aristotle "the philosopher," and he attempted to synthesize Aristotelian philosophy with the principles of Christianity. These teachings contributed to the rise of a specialized medical profession that treats the problem without regard to its effect on the whole person.

A Typical Example of a Western Mind-set

I was once having a conversation with my father, who is very much affected by the Western mind-set. He loves God and constantly prays for our spiritual nourishment and protection. He constantly prayed for us to grow in the Lord and love Him with all our hearts. At the age of twenty-seven, he experienced severe betrayal from close friends in the workplace. This experience caused major stress and anxiety. Later, he was diagnosed with diabetes. Now, because he had suffered from diabetes for the last thirty-nine years, his eyesight was deteriorating rapidly and he needed regular injections in the eyes to maintain his sight. Those injections were extremely painful, and for some reason they were not bringing the promised and expected effects to my father's eyes.

My father was sharing his disappointment with us, and as we were hearing him I found myself saying, "Dad, have you ever prayed for God to heal your eyesight?"

He answered, "No, because it is a result of my diabetes, and I have had it for many years, so it is a natural effect, plus I focus more on the spiritual stuff."

I explained to him, "Dad, God is concerned with all of you—spirit, soul, and body. It is great that you are going to the doctors, but why don't you pray for your healing also?" It was like a revelation for him. I explained to him that, "Many came to Jesus with physical illness, and He healed them all and did not tell them, 'I am more concerned with spirituality than your physical being.' In fact, on the cross, Jesus paid the price for your healing, and you need to claim what Jesus redeemed."

He was very convinced and agreed. He asked us to start praying for the healing of his eyes because the eye injections were extremely painful and his eyes were not showing any improvement. We laid our hands on his eyes and continued to pray each time his injections were due. Eventually, he contacted us as he left the doctor's surgery in amazement. The doctor had told him, "I have great news for you. Those injections were only meant to slow the rapid loss of sight, and for some reason your body was not responding well to them. However, recently your eyesight has been dramatically improving and that's not the usual."

My father had to break the news. He told the doctor, "I combined prayer with the treatment." My father needed to get set free from the Western mind-set. He needed to understand that God is interested in both our physical condition and our spiritual condition. The two should not be divorced from each other.

THE EASTERN MIND-SET

The Eastern mind-set is quite different from the Western mind-set. In it, sickness and healing are viewed in spiritual terms, affecting every aspect of the body. The causes of disease and the means of healing are not immediate and material but ultimate and spiritual, involving gods, ancestors, dreams, spells, traditional herbs, and "good and bad" spirits—as in white or black magic. People are at the mercy of a relational universe in which sickness is due to offended powers and healing is due to appeasement of the gods through rituals as sacrifices. Healing is mediated through the holy man, the shaman, spirit medium, witch doctor, or mystic. This leads to the use of alternative medicines, such as acupuncture and homeopathy (which are faith-based). These involve working with energy fields or *chakras*—the divine in us. They believe that healing comes by balancing auras, balancing or releasing energies, using crystals or magnetic rocks, practicing yoga, and transcendental meditation.

Sadly, the Eastern view is far from Christianity, and many Christians are affected by it. When they get sick, they think God must be upset with them due to something they must have done wrong, and God is trying to discipline them for their misdeeds. The most common answer is when people refer to Job or Paul's thorn in the flesh. (These topics will be discussed in further detail in my next book dealing with hindrances of healing.) Others quote and misunderstand the following verse:

> He said, "If you listen carefully to the Lord your God and do what is right in His eyes, if you pay attention to his commands and keep all his decrees, I will not bring on you any of the diseases I brought on the Egyptians, for I am the Lord, who heals you" (Exodus 15:26).

Their understanding of this verse is that God is the one who inflicts sickness on His people as a result of their disobedience and healing when they obey. Therefore, sickness and healing are based on works, not faith. They completely miss the fact that these instructions were written under the Mosaic covenant. In this covenant, God promised to make the Israelites His treasured possession among all people *if* they followed God's law. The form of the covenant resembles a suzerainty treaty in the ancient Near East. This treaty has a stronger party (suzerain) and a lesser party (vassal). The suzerain would document previous events in which they did a favor that benefitted the vassal. Here we see God telling the Israelites that He brought them out of the land of Egypt. The purpose of this would be to show that the more powerful party (God) was merciful and giving; therefore, the vassal should obey the stipulations that are presented in the treaty. In this case, the stipulations are total obedience and loyalty by the vassal (the people of Israel) to the suzerain (God). Total obedience results in blessings; disobedience results in curses (Deuteronomy 28:1-14; 28:14-68). The great news is that Christ has become the perfect sacrifice to atone for our sins, and He initiated a new covenant based on faith.

A Typical Example of an Eastern Mind-set

One on occasion, I was invited to speak at a church in New York. Many came out for prayers, and God did many amazing things. As I was leaving the church, my husband called me to pray for a lady with a paralyzed arm. I noticed that she didn't come up for prayer. I took her aside and was asking her why she didn't come out for prayer. She said, "I have committed many sins, and I know that God has paralyzed my arm so I can pay the price for my wrongdoing."

I was shocked, and explained to her, "Jesus paid the price for your sins and your sickness, and if you have received Him in your heart, then your sins are forgiven and by His stripes you have been healed." This was a revelation to her. We prayed for her to receive Jesus in her heart and declared that on the cross He paid the full price of her sins and sickness.

Immediately after prayer, she was made completely whole and was in tears. She was shouting at the top of her lungs, saying, *"He healed me, I am healed!"* Her husband was an atheist and had attended on this day to watch what we were going to do. When he saw what had happened to his wife, he believed. Later I found out that they started a weekly prayer group in their house and started to gather many people and share the message of the good news with those people.

BIBLICAL UNDERSTANDING

Now that we have considered the Western mind-set and the Eastern mind-set, it is about time to look at the biblical understanding of sickness and healing. One key verse would be Third John 1:2:

> *Beloved, I pray that you may prosper in all things and be in health, just as your soul prospers* (NKJV).

John greets his friend Gaius with a common Jewish blessing: "May you be prosperous and healthy," in a holistic sense—inwardly, bodily, socially, and materially. This implies an interrelated understanding of human nature, based on the Hebraic worldview of peace or shalom, which is God's holistic peace and prosperity, health and harmony experienced through the right relationship with God.

Beginning with Adam and Eve, we see throughout the Bible how a fractured relationship between God (who is the source), ourselves, each other, and creation led to the "curse," which is the chaos of sin, sickness, demons, and death. We also see that a restored relationship (reconciliation) through the Messiah's life, death, and resurrection breaks the curse and leads to forgiveness, healing, freedom, and eternal life. *Shalom* is God's reign of holistic order and well-being, which is the opposite of disintegration and destruction.

Biblical Understanding of Sickness

A biblical understanding of human disease is *disease*—a lack of ease in the whole person. Sicknesses are disorders, the opposite of shalom, a disruption of God's holistic harmony and relational well-being in the human being. Disease is a result of human sin, Adam's original disobedience. The curse of death intruded and spread throughout all creation.

> *When Adam sinned, sin entered the world. Adam's sin brought death, so death spread to everyone, for everyone sinned* (Romans 5:12 NLT).

As death is an intruder in God's creation, so sickness is not natural to human beings. Sickness is the foretaste of and curse of death. It is at war with us and our world in a destructively holistic sense.

Biblical Understanding of Healing

Healing is the event or process of restoring wholeness to the whole person. Healing is God's shalom, order, and well-being. The New Testament word for healing is "salvation," which is God's work in saving us and creation from sin, sickness, demons, and death. Such healing can only come to us, both immediately and ultimately, through the life, death, and resurrection of Jesus Christ by the power of the Holy Spirit. That's why we speak of divine healing and not faith healing.

> *For God was in Christ, reconciling the world to himself, no longer counting people's sins against them. And he gave us this wonderful message of reconciliation. So we are Christ's ambassadors; God is making his appeal through us. We speak for Christ when we plead, "Come back to God!" For God made Christ, who never sinned, to be the offering for our sin, so that we could be made right with God through Christ* (2 Corinthians 5:19-21 NLT).

It is very crucial that we are grounded in this biblical understanding. We have been made right with God, and sin has been atoned for. The price for our salvation, freedom, and healing has been paid in full. We freely receive it; however, this reconciliation has been extremely costly—it cost God His only beloved Son. Our core message is the ministry of reconciliation. When the Holy Spirit connects with our spirit, we get saved. When the Holy Spirit connects with our soul, we get delivered, and when the Holy Spirit connects with our body, we get healed.

As a result, we become Christ's ambassadors. God is making His appeal through us. We speak for Christ, the one who saves, heals, and delivers. He has paid the price for the whole person and is interested in our physical condition as well as our spiritual condition. He doesn't require us to perform certain acts to receive our healing or punish us for lack of performance. He is not upset with us; rather, He loves us like He loves His dear Son Jesus and is willing to give us all things (Romans 8:32).

Twice yearly, our team ministers in a national festival called MBS, which stands for Mind, Body, and Spirit. Many exhibitors from different faith groups such as Buddhists, Hindus, Muslims, and new age set up their stalls to sell products and offer different services. At the back of the hall, we find all the spirit mediums, the tarot card readers, and the palm readers. The line-up is massive, and they charge a substantial amount of money. We have been going to this dark place for many years now. We go to share God's unconditional love and truth. Many are reconciled to the Lord, and it is glorious to see them saved, healed, and delivered.

On one occasion, I had a very sick lady walk into our stand. Due to her understanding of karma, she had done many wrong things, and, as a result, karma was coming back at her. She said, "I am full of negative energy and for me to get healed, I must release the negative energy and replace it with positive energy."

I asked her a tough question. I said, "How do you release the negative energy?" She mentioned that she needs to go and visit an energy healer to release this energy. I had the honor of explaining to her the biblical understanding of sickness and healing. I explained to her that the wages of sin is eternal death, and that sickness is a result of sin. "For God made Jesus, who never sinned, to be the offering for our sin, so that we can be made right with God, and that when we connect with Him, we receive forgiveness of sin, healing of disease, freedom from evil spirits, and eternal life." She was full of joy and decided to receive Jesus. She was saved, healed, and delivered.

Chapter 6

IS HEALING IN THE ATONEMENT?

Let me start by sharing one of my favorite stories, which will explain this chapter clearly. I remember hearing the story of a very poor man who needed to travel on a cruise ship to get to a particular destination. He saved enough money to just get on the ship, and he packed a small bag of biscuits, cheese, and jam to just get by during his time of travel. Once this poor man boarded the ship, he spent most of his time in his cabin. Every morning he was handed the daily activities of the ship. There was amazing food, exciting shows, and many offshore excursions. Each day, he heard the passengers laughing and singing as they walked through the hallways, while he stayed in his cabin eating biscuits, cheese, and jam.

Finally, the ship arrived at his desired destination, and, as he was getting off, the captain of the ship was greeting the passengers. The captain said to him, "I hope you enjoyed the cruise and the program we put together." The poor man explained to the captain that he was very poor and didn't have extra cash to enjoy the food, shows, and entertainment. Sadness covered the captain's face, and he said to the man, "Sir, your entry ticket included *everything.*" The poor man was in absolute shock, feeling how his misunderstanding had robbed him of so much.

Just like this poor man, many Christians live life with the understanding that the atoning death of Christ on the cross only provides forgiveness of sin and eternal life. They have no problem believing and preaching that God is willing to forgive all sins, no matter how big or small they are. However, they have a big problem believing that the atoning death of Christ on the cross also heals every disease, that the same ticket which takes us to heaven includes the forgiveness of sin as well as the healing of diseases.

Sin is the root cause of sickness. The Bible clearly tells us that through Adam's disobedience, sin entered the world and death entered with it and spread to all people (2 Corinthians 5:12). Sin resulted in the curse and brought in sickness, demons, and eternal death. However, through Christ's obedience the curse is reversed, and we have been declared in right standing with God (2 Corinthians

5:19). His death brought forgiveness of sin, healing, freedom from demons, and eternal life.

Once I started to understand that on the cross Jesus paid the full price for my sickness and disease, I started to rebuke sickness and receive my healing. The apostle Paul is helping us to understand a simple equation. If sin is the root cause of sickness and Jesus atoned (paid the price) for my sin, then I should receive my healing, because sickness is a side effect of sin. However, many believers don't pray for their healing or claim it because they don't believe that it was part of what Christ paid for on the cross. They believe that the primary reason Jesus died on the cross was to forgive their sins so they can get to heaven, instead of getting heaven into them through healing and deliverance. It is about time we understand what exactly Jesus paid for, and what is included in the contract of salvation that is freely offered to us by our loving Father.

THE CROSS OF CHRIST

Isaiah 53 is considered one of the most direct and powerful Messianic prophecies related to the cross of Christ.

He was despised and rejected by mankind, a man of suffering, and familiar with pain. Like one from whom people hide their faces he was despised, and we held him in low esteem (Isaiah 53:3).

The word for "suffering" in Hebrew is *makob,* which can be translated as "pain." The word for "pain" in the Hebrew is *choliy,* which is translated as "sickness" or "disease."

> *Surely he took up our pain and bore our suffering, yet we considered him punished by God, stricken by him, and afflicted* (Isaiah 53:4).

The word for "took up" in Hebrew is *nasah.* It means "to lift from or carry away." The word for "pain" in Hebrew is *choliy* again, meaning "sickness and disease." The Hebrew word for "carried" is *sabal,* which means "to carry, bear the weight of" our sorrows. The Hebrew word for "suffering" is again *makob,* which means "pain."

He lifted up our sickness and diseases, and he carried our pain (Isaiah 53:5). Now let's see how physical healing is included in Isaiah 53.

In Matthew 8, Jesus performs many physical healings. The chapter starts with Jesus healing a man with leprosy (Matthew 8:1-4), followed by the healing of the centurion's manservant. This man felt that he wasn't worthy for Jesus to come under his roof, but he did understand the meaning of authority. The man asked Jesus to speak a word from wherever He was and his servant would be healed. Jesus spoke the word and the servant was healed (Matthew 8:5-13). The third physical healing in this same chapter was the healing of Peter's mother-in-law, who was lying in bed with a fever. Jesus touched her, and the fever immediately left her and she got up and waited on them (Matthew 8:14-15). Word about Jesus' healing went out, and when evening came He healed all the sick and drove out evil spirits (Matthew 8:16). Matthew tells us that these healings are a fulfillment of what the prophet Isaiah prophesied in chapter 53.

> *When evening came, many who were demon-possessed were brought to him, and he drove out the spirits with a word and healed all the sick. This was to fulfill what was spoken through the prophet Isaiah: "He took up our infirmities and bore our diseases"* (Matthew 8:16-17).

Matthew declared that when Jesus healed all these people, He was fulfilling the Messianic prophecy of Isaiah 53. He walked around lifting off people's infirmities and carrying off their sickness and disease. The apostle Peter explains to us that on the cross, Jesus carried our sins in His body, and once again he references Isaiah 53:5, which tells us that *"by his wounds we are healed."* In other words, Jesus on the cross has fully paid the price for your sins. The root cause of sickness was dealt with at the cross. It was paid in full. For the Bible tells us that *"God made him who had no sin to be sin for us, so that in him we might become the righteousness of God"* (2 Corinthians 5:21).

When we unite with Jesus, we become the righteousness of God. In other words, the Father sees us the same way He sees Jesus. We become in right standing with God—fully redeemed, justified, forgiven, and healed. Jesus is not holding back my healing and waiting until I perform religious duties to release it. He has fully paid for it, and my role is to receive by faith what Christ has paid for. I am not required to beg God to heal me or to remind God how much I deserve my healing. I need to know that when I received Jesus into my heart, I received His salvation, His healing, and His freedom all at the same time. When Jesus moved into my heart, He moved all His work with Him. God is not holding back anything from me. In actual fact, the Bible tells us that God *"who did not spare his own Son, but gave him up for us all—how will he not also, along with him, graciously give us all things?"* (Romans 8:32).

With this understanding in mind, the cross of Christ does not become a reflection of our sins but of our value. On this cross, Christ disarmed the demonic powers and authorities and made a public spectacle of them, triumphing over them by the cross (Colossians 2:15). The cross of Christ is the *dunamis* power of God to save, heal, and deliver. This power has already been released, and just like I receive my salvation by faith, I also receive my healing by faith. If I believe that Jesus is able to forgive all sins, then I must also believe that He is able to heal all sickness. My role is to receive, not achieve. I can't do anything beyond what Jesus did to achieve my healing, because my healing has been paid for and released. The verse "by his stripes I have been healed" is actually past tense. Healing was already paid for and released at the cross.

I was reminded of the story of a father who purchased a four-wheel-drive vehicle. The vehicle was spacious and comfortable to drive. He was thankful about having air conditioning in the vehicle, as well as being able to hear music. Sometime after, his son needed to borrow the vehicle for a few days to attend a work conference. When he returned the vehicle to his father, the father was surprised. He said to his son, "The seats are warm, and the navigation system has voice commands." The father asked the son, "When did you install these extra features?"

The son was surprised and said, "Dad, I didn't install anything. Everything was already there, but you just didn't know it."

The father said, "I was in the snowy mountains many times, and wished to have these features."

The son said, "Dad, they all come as standard with this vehicle. You just didn't know what you had." Sadly, this is the situation with many Christians today. Healing comes standard with the cross of Christ. The cross of Christ includes salvation, healing, freedom, and eternal life.

THE BRONZE SNAKE

The bronze snake in the Book of Numbers, chapter 21, is another great story that points to the cross and its relationship to divine healing. The people of Israel had left Egypt, and now they were in the wilderness, heading toward the Promised Land. They had to take the longer route to the Red Sea because the King of Edom denied them entry. The people became impatient with the long journey, and they began to speak against God and Moses. As a result, a plague of poisonous snakes bit and killed many. When Moses prayed, the Lord told him:

"Make a *replica of a poisonous snake and attach it to a pole. All who are bitten will live if they simply look at it!*" So Moses made a snake out of bronze and attached it to a pole. Then anyone who was bitten by a snake could look at the bronze snake and be healed! (Numbers 21:8-9 NLT)

The very thing (the snake) that had caused the deaths needed to die in order for the people to receive their healing by faith. The people who were bitten were not asked to perform extra duties other than "look at the pole" with the snake on it. The Bible clearly tells us that sin is the root cause of our sickness, and when sin dies healing is received. We also know that we all have sinned and come short of the glory of God (Romans 3:23); that's why God sent His own Son in the likeness of sinful flesh to be a sin offering. And so He condemned sin in the flesh (Romans 8:3).

Jesus referred to the story of the bronze snake when He was speaking to Nicodemus in John 3. Nicodemus was a Jewish religious leader and a Pharisee. Due to fear of the Pharisees, he approached Jesus when it was dark to learn more and ask Him some questions. Jesus told him a shocking statement, *"Unless you are born again, you cannot see the Kingdom of God!"* (John 3:3 NLT). Nicodemus could not understand what Jesus meant and didn't know how to enter the Kingdom. Nicodemus was a Pharisee and well educated in religious law, so Jesus used the story of the bronze snake in the Book of Numbers to explain to him.

> *Just as Moses lifted up the snake in the wilderness, so the Son of Man must be lifted up, that everyone who believes may have eternal life in him* (John 3:14).

Jesus is making it clear that just like Moses lifted up the poisonous snake in the wilderness, and every bitten person who looked at the snake was healed, so the Son of Man will also be lifted on a pole and everyone who believes in Him will have eternal life—that is, salvation. In the Old Testament, those who looked at the bronze snake were physically healed. In the New Testament, those who believe in Him have eternal life. They are healed, saved, and delivered.

One of the most powerful statements ever made by Jesus is *"It is finished"* (John 19:30). The Greek tense indicates that the work of redemption has been completed once and for all by Jesus Christ and its results are abiding continuously. The resurrection of Christ is the most important event in the Bible, because it is the evidence that the Father has fully accepted the sacrifice of the Son. Sin has totally been atoned for, and we now have peace with God. All Christ has paid for is now our inheritance through adoption. We have become sons and daughters to a loving Father who didn't spare His own Son for us, but with Him gave us all things.

At this point, many will start to ask, "If Christ paid for our healing at the cross, then why don't many believers get healed?" This is a difficult question, and before I attempt to answer it, we must agree to elevate the work of the cross and the promises of God above personal experiences, not the other way around. We have prayed for many believers who were not immediately healed due to wrong beliefs about healing. For example, some believe that God sent this sickness to discipline them. As a result, they don't want to go against God's work, and therefore they don't get healed. However, once their mind is renewed and they understand that God is a good Father who will only give good gifts to His children, then they start to rebuke the sickness and receive God's healing into their body.

I remember meeting a beautiful young bride who was diagnosed with stage four cancer. Unfortunately, she was raised to believe that sickness is from God to bring you closer to Him. While we prayed many times and rebuked the cancer, on the inside she had a deep belief that her cancer was from God. On the last day of her life, I went to the hospital and prayed for her. I remember rebuking the cancer and doing all I knew to get her healed. Sadly, she passed away. She was married to a lovely young man who was an atheist, and he said, "If Jesus heals her, I will believe in Him."

I was begging God to move and heal her. But unfortunately, she died. I was broken for a long time and was asking God about it. I said, "God, I asked You to heal her. Why didn't You?"

The answer was shocking. I heard God say, *"There is nothing more I can do than what I have done. I have paid for her healing and released it."*

The young woman didn't fully receive this healing into her body due to the beliefs that she held on to. At this time, I remembered Dr. Randy Clark's words: "You don't take the glory, and you don't take the blame. Your role is to pray, and His role is to heal."

Since that day, I have decided to pray for all those who need healing and to try and explain to them that healing is included in the cross of Christ. I get very excited when people get healed, but I have trained myself to keep going even when people don't. Human beings are complex, and we approach God with so much baggage, which sometimes blocks our healing. That's why renewing our mind is very important. We learn that Jesus is our model and great example, and we humbly follow what He said and trust Him with the results. Many times we pray for people, and nothing happens immediately. Then we suggest that they go home and declare the promises of the Lord over their lives, and suddenly they get healed.

Setting the foundation is more important than receiving our healing. Knowing what Christ paid for is very essential for our journey. Jesus loved us all the way and has made a provision for us so we can live an abundant life. The more we uphold His promises and trust His word more than what our eyes see, the more we will see His glory manifest in amazing ways.

Chapter 7

IS IT GOD'S WILL TO HEAL AT ALL TIMES?

This chapter is foundational in helping us discover the will of God for healing. Many people do not really know the will of God with regard to healing. Some believe that it is not God's will to heal at all times. Others believe that God is sovereign, and, as a result, He will heal some and not others. These different views make it very difficult for us to receive our healing. If I truly believe that sometimes the will of God is not to heal someone, then how can I possibly ask for that person to be healed? If I did, I would be going against God's will.

I remember once visiting my sick grandfather in the hospital. As I entered the hospital, a young man, whose wife was hospitalized in one of the hospital wards, approached me. He recognized me from our weekly television program and asked me to pray for his wife. I agreed, and we went upstairs to find her. Getting to know her, I found out that they have four beautiful children and that she was diagnosed with a rare blood disease and wasn't given much hope to live. I explained to her that I was here for prayer and that I believed Jesus wanted to heal her. She agreed, and we started praying for her healing.

As I started to rebuke the sickness and disease, I felt great resistance and heard her mumbling some stuff. As I paid closer attention to what she was saying, I heard her say, "I want Your will, God, only Your will, only what You want."

At this moment, I stopped praying and asked her, "Do you believe that God's will is for you to be healed?"

She replied, "I don't know, because I have received prayer many times and wasn't healed. I don't want anything against His will." I took the time to explain to her how to know what the will of God is. She was very convinced and came into agreement with the will of God instead of questioning it.

The best way to know the will of God is to look at Jesus. He is the author and the finisher of our faith (Hebrews 12:2). Jesus' most important assignment was not only to save us, but to also reveal the Father's heart. He clearly said, "*I have come down from heaven to do the will of God who sent me, not to do my own will"* (John 6:38 NLT). Everything Jesus did and taught was to reveal the Father to us. The Gospel of John clearly tells us that no one has ever seen God. But the unique one, who is Himself God (that is Jesus), has revealed God to us (John 1:18). The apostle Paul describes Jesus to the people of Colossae by telling them that Christ is the visible image of the invisible God (Colossians 1:15). In other words, to really know the will of the Father, we need to focus on the ministry of Jesus and ask ourselves a question. When did Jesus deny anyone their healing by telling them that it is not the Father's will or it is not the Father's timing or even that the Father is trying to teach them something through this sickness? The Bible clearly tells us that He healed everyone who was brought to Him.

> *A large crowd followed him, and he healed all who were ill* (Matthew 12:15).
>
> *At sunset, the people brought to Jesus all who had various kinds of sickness, and laying his hands on each one, he healed them* (Luke 4:40).
>
> *Great crowds came to him, bringing the lame, the blind, the crippled, the mute and many others, and laid them at his feet; and he healed them* (Matthew 15:30).

In these essential verses, we see Jesus healing multitudes, without ever mentioning to anyone that God's will is for them to be sick. On the contrary, when Philip asked

Jesus to show him the Father, Jesus said to him, *"Anyone who has seen me has seen the Father"* (John 14:9). Jesus continues to tell Philip that *"The words I speak are not my own, but my Father who lives in me does His work through me"* (John 14:10 NLT). The "work" he is referring to is healing the sick and casting out demons. This verse tells us that it was the Father living in Jesus who actually healed the sick. He demonstrated His will through Christ by healing.

Another great healing encounter that truly demonstrates God's will to heal is found in the following story. Although the story is short, one can easily miss the magnitude of its greatness due to the lacking cultural understanding of the time.

> *A man with leprosy came and knelt in front of Jesus, begging to be healed. "If you are willing, you can heal me and make me clean," he said. Moved with compassion, Jesus reached out and touched him. "I am willing," he said. "Be healed!" Instantly the leprosy disappeared, and the man was healed* (Mark 1:40-42 NLT).

In Jesus' day, leprosy referred to various contagious skin diseases. Leprosy was caused by a type of bacteria that attacks the nervous system, grossly deforming and slowly rotting the flesh. According to Luke's account, this man was *"covered with leprosy"* (Luke 5:12). Josephus, who was a first-century historian, said lepers were treated "as if they were, in effect, dead people." The Torah gave strict laws governing the quarantining of lepers outside the walls of cities and towns due to their "defilement." In those days, those who suffered from a serious skin disease must tear their clothing and leave their hair uncombed. They must cover their mouths and call out, *"Unclean! Unclean!"* (Leviticus 13:45). The penalty for entering a city or town was forty lashes. Physical contact with a leper brought serious spiritual, ceremonial, and social defilement.

Leprosy had destroyed this man spiritually, mentally, emotionally, physically, and socially. When this leper saw Jesus, he came to Him, revealing his desperation and faith; he knelt down, fell with his face to the ground, and begged Jesus for healing. He broke all the religious and social taboos. Given all the above, it is astonishing that he even dared to come to this rabbi—unless the more astonishing reputation of Jesus' radical compassion and healing power had preceded Him. Just like many of us, this leper believed Jesus was able to heal him, but he was not sure if Jesus was willing to heal him. This is common when it comes to physical healing. Most people believe that God is able to heal them, but the question comes in, "Is He willing to heal me now?" So many of us bargain with God; we question God: "Lord, if You are willing, if I am worthy enough. If I fast and pray and serve the poor, will You heal me?" We can't bargain with God. We need to believe *both* His ability and His loving will to heal as a gift of grace and mercy.

Jesus' response was amazing. He moved with compassion for the man and was angry at the leprosy. That moved Him into action. He did the unthinkable, going against Torah prohibitions and social stigma. Rather than the flow of the defilement entering Jesus, healing went from Jesus into the man, which was the greater power residing in Him. Jesus indicated His willingness to heal by touching the man, but He also gave verbal assurance of His willingness to heal the man. In so doing, Jesus presented the Father's essential nature—healing is God's will for people. This was very different and contrary to the way other rabbis portrayed God. Those rabbis believed that leprosy was defilement, even punishment from God. Jesus used His authority and spoke the word of healing, releasing God's power.

One might argue that it could have been God's will to heal this leper, but that doesn't really mean that God wants to heal everyone. If this is the case, then the story in Luke 17:11-19 sheds a different light. In this story, as Jesus reaches the border between Galilee and Samaria, ten lepers stand at a distance, calling out, *"Jesus, Master, have mercy on us!"* (Luke 17:13 NLT). Jesus simply tells them to perform an act of obedience. He asks them to go and show themselves to the priests.

The priests were in Jerusalem, which is a long distance to travel. Normally, when people got healed from a skin disease, they went to show themselves to the priest. The priest then examined them, and if they had been healed, they would be asked to offer the appropriate sacrifices and be pronounced clean. In this case, none of the lepers were healed yet, but they needed to go to the priest by faith. The Bible tells us that as they as went, they were cleansed from their leprosy (Luke 17:14).

However, focusing on the will of God, we don't see Jesus personally interviewing them and telling them, "It is God's will to heal two; the rest will just die." On the contrary, Jesus didn't ask any questions; He simply gave them all the same opportunity to get healed. This shows God's radical desire to heal. Surely not all the ten lepers were righteous; surely not all the lepers were at peace with everyone. But we do see that they all moved in faith, and all were healed. For us to effectively pray for people and see results, we need to be absolutely certain that God's will is to heal at all times. If we are not certain of God's will, then how will we effectively rebuke sickness and unite with God to receive our healing? From those two examples I have just used, it is clear that God's will is for us to be healed.

The question here becomes, "Do I want to be healed?" Many might think that this is a silly question and that no one wants to get sick. However, this is not the case for many people. I was once praying with an elderly woman who was quite ill. She asked for prayer for her spiritual life but not her physical illness. When I asked if she wanted prayer, she refused and thanked me. As I got to know her better, I found out that she had two children who were quite busy with their lives and neglected her. When they heard of her sickness, they made the effort to visit her regularly and stay in touch. This poor woman feared that if she was healed, her children would slip back into their old habits and that she would miss out on seeing them. As a result, she wanted to stay sick so that she could see her children regularly.

Sometimes people receive particular financial benefits from the government for their disability. Getting healed means losing those benefits. Once again, those people might come for prayer, but deep on the inside they are holding on to their sickness. We meet a similar man inside the city near the sheep gate, which was the pool of Bethesda (John 5:2). Many sick people who were blind, lame, and paralyzed surrounded this particular man. He had been lame for thirty-eight years. When Jesus knew he was lying there for such a long time, He asked him a very strange question. He asked him, *"Would you like to get well?"* (John 5:6 NLT). One would think this is an invalid question. Of course, he wants to get well. But Jesus knew that just because someone is sick, it doesn't mean they want to get well.

Interestingly, this man came up with an excuse for why he wasn't healed. In his mind, an angel of the Lord would come down at times and stir the water. The first person in the water after the angel stirred it got healed. Although this method didn't work for him, he never pursued a different method. His excuses were that he didn't have anyone who cared enough to put him in the water after the angel stirred it. He found a reason to hold on to his sickness. The Bible doesn't mention this man's name other than "the invalid." The length of time of his sickness and his surrounding sick friends defined who he was. Even when Jesus Himself approached him, he didn't ask to be healed. Here we get to see Jesus' radical desire to heal. Although this man didn't give a straight answer and didn't ask for Jesus to heal him, he was healed.

We know that the root cause for this man's sickness was his sin. Some might think that unless you repent, you won't be healed. Jesus used a different model and didn't impose any conditions on people. He healed this man and later gave him a command to stop sinning (John 5:14). His compassion and extravagant love and kindness are the reasons people repent (Romans 2:4). Sometimes we play God and refuse to pray for people who we know have sin in their lives. Or we teach people that if there is sin in their lives, God won't heal them. The truth is, while we were still sinners Christ died for us (Romans 5:8). He didn't wait until we repented to save us. The same is true about healing. God's love covers a multitude of sins (1 Peter 4:8).

This is not to say that we make a practice of sinning, for no one who abides in Him keeps on sinning (1 John 3:6). It is true that Jesus first healed this man before asking him to repent. However, it is also true that Jesus went back to him and asked him to stop sinning or something worse may happen to him (John 5:14). Jesus is not threatening the man to stop sinning or God will inflict him with a worse sickness. Jesus is simply asking him to "stop sinning." In other words, to close the door from which sickness entered, which is his flesh; otherwise, this door will be reopened through his sin, and he will get sicker. Jesus is simply dealing with the root cause of his sickness so that he is able to maintain his freedom and healing. Jesus is teaching us that healing is not simply an event; it is a process—a lifestyle of holiness and freedom.

Having laid the foundation, it is clear that God's will is to heal me, and it is His will to heal me now. So many people will repeat words such as, "I am waiting for the Lord's timing," when, in reality, God is waiting for us to come to Him and get our healing. We never see Jesus tell anyone to wait for the Lord's timing. The Lord's timing took place almost 2,000 years ago on the cross, and by His stripes we were healed. The Bible clearly teaches us that if two agree about something they ask for, it will be done for them (Matthew 18:19). When we agree with the will of the Father in Heaven, healing takes place. When we ask for His reign, His kingdom to come on earth as it is in Heaven, we release His presence and unite with His will. There is no sickness in heaven, there is no cancer in Heaven, there is no depression in Heaven. It is about time we agree with His will and release Heaven to invade earth.

Chapter 8

RECEIVE YOUR HEALING

THE NATURE OF GOD

Before discovering the different routes to healing, we first need to be grounded in the nature of God as our healer and explore the scope of His healing. Healing flows from the nature of God. Healing is not foreign to Him; it is who He is. Healing is His character. It is the attribute or feature that makes up His personality.

The Exodus from Egypt is God's greatest act of salvation in the Old Testament. During the Exodus, the people of Israel knew God to be the God who is all powerful, the God who is mighty in battle, the great warrior who fights for His people, the God who split the Red Sea and brought judgment upon the Egyptians. After their escape from Egypt, God knew that they would be wandering in the wilderness for forty years. He knew that there would be no hospitals or medical centers in the wilderness. As a result, God wanted to reveal to them His nature and extend His care and protection. He wanted to reveal to them who He was to them, and who He would be to them. Hence, He declared, *"I am the Lord, who heals you"* (Exodus 15:26).

As a result, three million people ended up traveling around the wilderness without ever getting sick. The Bible tells us that not one among them stumbled (Psalm 105:37); rather, the Lord kept them free from every disease (Deuteronomy 7:15). That's because it is His nature; He is the God who heals. His character is constant and never changes.

The Book of James clearly tells us that every good and perfect gift is from above, coming down from the Father of the heavenly lights who doesn't change like shifting shadows (James 1:17). God's nature and His character are constant. He only gives good gifts to His children. We need to be firmly grounded in who God is; otherwise, how can we expect Him to do something that He is not? In revealing the Father to us, Jesus said, *"If you, then, though you are evil, know how to give good gifts to your children, how much more will your Father in heaven give good gifts to those who ask him!"* (Matthew 7:11). Those powerful verses reveal the character of God as the God who heals and, more importantly, that this nature doesn't change with time; rather, He is the same yesterday, today, and forever (Hebrews 13:8). He healed and will always continue to heal. Unlike us, His position hasn't changed. Healing never ceased throughout church history. Just like evangelism—the more we evangelize, the more people get saved. Healing is the same—the more we pray for the sick, the more we will see them healed.

God's position on healing has not changed. We need to change our position to be in line with God. That's why Jesus said, *"The time has come. ...The kingdom of God has come near. Repent and believe the good news!"* (Mark 1:15). Mark is saying, "History has reached its climax! It is the day of the Lord! The prophecies of Israel's times and destiny are now being fulfilled." God has come to destroy evil, to save and heal Israel and the nations. The Pharisees would have heard, "The Messiah is here to overthrow the Romans!" But God was defeating a greater army—satan and his oppression. It means satan's end has come, and a new beginning is about to start.

King Jesus is the first and the last, the beginning and the end (Revelation 1:8). He is announcing the end of satan's reign of sin, sickness, demons, and death (judgment) and the beginning of new life, the restoration and recreation of all things. Therefore, we need to *repent* and *believe*. *Repentance* means more than turning from our sin. It means "change our mind," which is *meta-noia*—a paradigm shift. *Believe* means opening and entrusting ourselves to what God is doing. In other words, Mark is saying that God is actively present, asserting this kingship over all evil. In order to experience and receive this Kingdom, we need to change our mind-set and thinking and open ourselves to all God has for us.

THE SCOPE OF HEALING

When it comes to the scope of healing, I am reminded of King David, who said, *"Praise the Lord, my soul, and forget not all his benefits—who forgives all your sins and heals all your diseases"* (Psalm 103:2-3). While many of us know this verse quite well, we find it hard to believe. We have no problem believing that God is able to forgive all sins, no matter big or small they are. However, we find it challenging to believe that He is able to heal all sickness, especially physical illness. It is easier to minister healing to what is "unseen" (inner healing), as no one knows if the healing takes place or not—it is only observable later in attitudinal, behavioral changes.

In Mark 2, we come across a paralyzed man, who was carried by his four friends and brought to Jesus from the house roof. When Jesus saw their faith, He said to the paralyzed man, *"Son, your sins are forgiven"* (Mark 2:5). Sin was the root cause of this man's paralysis, and it needed to be forgiven and removed in order for this man to be healed. Because the forgiveness of sin is unseen, the teachers of the law were angry with Jesus and accused Him of blaspheming. That is why Jesus asked them, *"Which is easier: to say to this paralyzed man, 'Your sins are forgiven* [which is unseen],*' or to say, 'Get up* [which is seen], *take your mat and walk'?"* (Mark 2:9). It is obvious that the harder one is the one that is seen, because if the healing doesn't take place the credibility of the healer is in doubt.

Immediately, Jesus commanded the man to get up, take his mat, and go home. No one saw whether God forgave the man's sin, but everyone saw when he picked up his bed and walked. The proof that the sins were really forgiven was the physical healing of this man. As a result, the Bible tells us that this amazed everyone, and they praised God, saying, *"We have never seen anything like this!"* (Mark 2:12).

Physical healing is tangible and verifiable, so some might find it challenging to minister. However, we need to remember that healing (inner healing as well as physical healing) is a Kingdom event. The future resurrection breaks into our bodies, defeating satan's rule of mortal sickness on the basis of Jesus' defeat of satan in His physical life, death, and resurrection. On that basis, God is able to heal physically as well as emotionally. He is able to heal every sickness and disease, despite the name we give to the disease.

I remember once ministering healing to a friend who was diagnosed with stage four breast cancer. She was full of peace and hope. She said to me, "When I was first diagnosed with the disease, I was shattered, and couldn't believe that I was diagnosed with stage four cancer. Doctors literally gave me a month to live. When I went for my treatment, I became fearful and very depressed as I watched patients suffer and share their stories." She said, "I had no one to go to but the Lord. I started praying, and opened the Bible randomly to find the most amazing passage." This brought so much peace, joy, and hope to her mind and heart. It was the apostle Paul's prayer to the Ephesians. He prayed that the believers would be enlightened to know about the hope of His calling, the riches of His glorious inheritance, and His incomparably great power for the believers. That power is exactly the same as the power He exerted when He raised Christ from the dead and seated Him at His right hand, far above all rule and authority, power and dominion, and every name that is invoked, not only in the present age, but also in the one to come, and that God placed all things under the authority of Christ and appointed Him head over everything (Ephesians 1:18-22).

This passage brought to her such a revelation—that the name of Jesus and the power of His spirit is far above all rule and authority, power and dominion, and every name that is invoked. His name is higher than "stage four cancer" and higher than all negative reports. His name is higher than all expectation and stipulations. In fact, God has placed "stage four cancer" under the authority of Christ. This revelation changed everything. She knew that God had raised her with Christ and seated her in the heavenly realms in Christ Jesus (Ephesians 2:6). This revelation made all the difference. She started to pray from heaven to earth instead of from earth to heaven. She prayed from the throne room and knew that the name of her condition was fully under the feet of Christ, that His name was higher and mightier than all names that are invoked throughout all the ages. We need a revelation to keep going and to correctly understand where sickness is positioned and where God is positioned.

HEALING COMES THROUGH DIFFERENT ROUTES

All genuine healings ultimately come from God. He heals primarily, though not exclusively, through human and natural means, including natural and scientific medicines and healthy lifestyles. However, in terms of Christian ministry, God heals the body in answer to prayer and faith through the laying on of hands and speaking God's Word.

The Laying on of Hands

Jesus healed many with the laying on of hands. He commissioned believers to do the same. The only qualification to have is to believe.

> *And these signs will accompany those who believe: In my name they will drive out demons; they will speak in new tongues; they will pick up snakes with their hands; and when they drink deadly poison, it will not hurt them at all; they will place their hands on sick people, and they will get well* (Mark 16:17-18).

Your hands become His hands—His tool! The power of the Holy Spirit flows through your hands. In this case, the believer lays his hands on the unbeliever. In the Book of Acts chapter 3, Peter and John came across a lame beggar. Peter knew what he carried before attempting to heal the man. He said to him, *"Silver or gold I do not have, but what I do have I give you. In the name of Jesus Christ of Nazareth, walk"* (Acts 3:6). Before laying our hands on someone, we need to know what we are carrying and that when we lay on our hands we are transferring the power of the resurrected Christ who lives inside of us. We need to acknowledge that the

Spirit of Him (God) who raised Jesus from the dead is living in us (Romans 8:11).

Through the Spoken Word

Many times, Jesus healed by a word of command. To the man whose hand was shriveled, He said, *"Stretch out your hand"* (Luke 6:10). To the centurion whose servant lay at home paralyzed, He said, *"Go! Let it be done just as you believed it would"* (Matthew 8:13). To the paralyzed man, whose friends brought him from the roof, He said, *"Get up"* (Mark 2:11). To the dead man in the city of Nain, He said, *"Arise"* (Luke 7:14 NKJV). Jesus rebuked sickness and demons, and His words carried power.

The apostle Paul followed Christ's model. The Bible tells us that in Lystra he met a man who had been lame since birth. This man was listening to Paul as he was preaching. Paul looked directly at him and saw that he had faith to be healed. He said to him, *"Stand up on your feet!"* (Acts 14:10). Just like our touch has power through the laying on of hands, our words carry power also. We can command our healing in Jesus' name. When we operate in the name of Jesus, we operate in His authority. We need to know that *"If anyone speaks, they should do so as one who speaks the very words of God"* (1 Peter 4:11). It is no longer we who speak, but Christ speaking through us. We are not commanding God to heal. God is on our side, and together with Him, we are commanding sickness and disease to leave; we are speaking to the body to be restored to full function. We need to understand that healing is a direct confrontation between the Spirit's power and material disorder and that our words carry the power to heal and restore.

God sends His Word to heal and rescue (Psalm 107:20). Healing can be instant, but it can also be gradual, as body tissue takes time to heal and recover. Meditating on God's Word is essential to healing. We know that faith comes by hearing—that is, hearing the Word of God (Romans 10:17). As we hear the Word, our minds are transformed to have the mind of Christ (1 Corinthians 2:16). Faith builds us on the inside, and we begin to take hold of God's promises and declare that by His stripes we have been healed. We start to believe that what is impossible to man is possible to God (Luke 18:27). It is time to soak in the Word, declare the Word, believe the Word, and speak the Word.

Through Communion

The apostle Paul is sharing a secret to healing through the communion.

> For those who eat and drink without discerning the body of Christ eat and drink judgment on themselves. That is why many among you are weak and sick, and a number of you have fallen asleep (1 Corinthians 11:29).

This is a very important perspective. There is healing in partaking in the "meal that heals." First, we need to notice that this is referring to the body, not the cup. If we take it without recognizing the Body of the Lord, it can lead to judgment. The cup represents the blood and the remission of sins. However, the body is where He bore our sicknesses and our diseases (Isaiah 53:4). When we do not discern what happened at the cross in the Body of Jesus for our healing, we become ignorant of what Christ has done.

When we take communion, we need to be reminded: "In His Body, He bore my disease. In His body, He bore my sickness. In His Body, He bore my sorrows." The word *sorrows* in the King James Version actually means "weakness," not "sadness."

We need to understand that through the blood there is forgiveness of sin, and every time we take communion we are reminded of that. However, we also need to discern that in His Δ113 He died, bearing our sickness and disease so that we can be healed. It is then that we can receive the grace for healing.

Through the Holy Spirit

Believers need to understand the power of the following verse.

And if the Spirit of him who raised Jesus from the dead is living in you, he who raised Christ from the dead will also give life to your mortal bodies because of his Spirit who lives in you (Romans 8:11).

In reality, when we receive Christ, we receive provision into our spirit for all we need. Every needed healing was deposited into our spirit the day we were born again. This power resides in our spirit and needs to reach our sick body. The passageway to release this power is through the soul. The soul (our mind, will, and emotions) is the passage through which this power comes. When our mind is not renewed, we can die with all this power stuck in our spirit, never reaching our sick bodies. We need to be grounded in this verse. We are not waiting for God to release His healing; He has already supplied us with everything we need. The Spirit of the Father who raised Jesus from the dead is living in us and is willing to give life to every dying cell on the inside of us.

Through Prayer

Prayer is very important when it comes to healing. John Wesley once said, "God does nothing except in response to believing prayer." The Book of James tells us exactly that.

Is anyone among you sick? Let them call the elders of the church to pray over them and anoint them with oil in the name of the Lord. And the prayer offered in faith will make the sick person well; the Lord will raise them up. If they have sinned, they will be forgiven (James 5:14-15).

Notice that when someone becomes sick, they are the ones who are meant to call for the elders. The elders are mature Christians who pray for the sick. When the elders come, they are meant to pray and anoint with oil. Notice that it is not the oil that heals; it is the prayer offered in faith that heals the sick. That encourages us to pray for the sick. If you are reading this book and you are sick, get different people to pray for you until you receive your healing.

Chapter 9

EXERCISING MY AUTHORITY

I n order to fight sickness and disease, we need to exercise our authority, which we have received from Christ. The most popular Greek word for "authority" is *exousia* (sometimes translated as "power"). This term is found 102 times in the New Testament. Many don't have a clear, solid understanding of their authority in Christ. Some think that Christ has ultimate authority and has given us partial authority, while others think that authority over the devil belongs only to a few chosen people to whom God has given special power.

The truth is, we receive this authority when we are born again.

As we are made new creatures in Christ Jesus, we inherit the Name of the Lord Jesus Christ, and we can use it in prayer against the enemy. In fact, when we use the name of Jesus, we operate in His full authority. For example, if we get pulled over by a policeman, he stops us in the name of the state, and we must obey even if he was employed that very morning. The fact is, if he is wearing a badge, he has full authority and we must submit to him.

Sadly, many don't understand the truth about their authority in Christ, and when they get sick they don't acknowledge that they are under attack. They think God is sovereign and He allowed this sickness to teach them something instead of realizing that this is not from God and they need to use the authority Christ entrusted to them to come up against it. Others say, "Well, maybe I gave the enemy authority over my life through an open door and that's why the enemy entered and brought in sickness." They start to blame themselves for something they have done and give the enemy a legal right through their words. Biblically, this understanding is incorrect. The enemy doesn't need your permission to enter in and bring sickness. The enemy is a thief and a liar. He doesn't wait for your authority to break in. He just does.

In addition to that, technically you don't even have the authority to give to the enemy. If you have surrendered the ownership of your life to the lordship of Christ, then you don't have authority over your life to start with, so how can you give it? The truth is, the minute you gave your heart to the Lord, you have become a target to the enemy. When you invited Christ into your life, you have moved from the dominion of darkness to the Kingdom of His beloved Son (Colossians 1:3). Your old boss found out you are working with his opposition and declares a war against you. We are not scared of the enemy because he was disarmed, and Christ made a public display of him by triumphing over him on the cross (Colossians 2:15). Satan knows he lost the battle, but will continue to lie, steal, kill, and destroy. That's why, as God's children, we need to take our stand against him and learn how to fight back.

Many experience spiritual attack from the enemy and cry out to God, expecting God to do something. They do not realize that Christ has defeated satan and taken all authority from him, and through union with Christ we are able to operate in His full authority. Soldiers train in the army, so they get ready for battle. During their army training, they get to learn and practice using machine guns, planes, and tanks. Can you imagine if during war they didn't know how to fight against the enemy? Can you imagine if they call their leaders in the army and say to them, "Our enemies are fast approaching. What do we do?" or "Can you help us?" Their leaders would be very disappointed and would tell them, "We can't do anything extra to help you. We already trained you and supplied you with all you need to fight the enemy. You just need to fight the enemy."

That's exactly our position—many don't know the magnitude of what Christ has done. They are ignorant of how to use their tools in warfare. We don't know what our authority is or how to use it. As a result, we don't think we are equipped enough to command or rebuke the enemy. We don't think our words carry much weight. We command the enemy to leave, and we get surprised when he does instead of getting surprised when he doesn't. It is time to wake up and understand the nature of the authority Christ has given us. It is time to learn how we use it and be confident that when we use the authority God gave us the devil must submit and obey.

God created the heavens and the earth in five days. On the sixth day, God created humankind in His image and likeness as the climax of His creation. God gave Adam and Eve full authority to care for creation. He blessed them and entrusted them to manage the earth by being fruitful and subduing it, by ruling over the fish, the birds, and all living creatures (Genesis 1:28). In Adam and Eve, we broke trust with God by sinning against Him. We gave away our God-given authority to satan. Having failed in his attempt to grasp the title deeds of heaven, satan came to earth to grab the title deeds from us. The earth and all on it came under "the curse" of satan's rule of sin, sickness, pain, poverty, demons, and death. Satan became *"the god of this age* [who] *has blinded the minds of unbelievers"* (2 Corinthians 4:4). Because we are made in God's image, Jesus of Nazareth is the nearest relative of every human being. Jesus came to save us from satan's tyranny. Jesus did not grasp at equality with God, neither did He use it to His advantage, as satan did. He stripped Himself of position, power, and glory and came to earth to buy us back (Philippians 2:7-11).

He began His ministry announcing the Kingdom, healing the sick, and delivering the imprisoned and enslaved of every disease and sickness (Matthew 4:23). He literally drove out satan from human bodies, which are God's territory. Jesus continued to travel throughout all towns and villages, teaching and announcing the Good News about the Kingdom of God, and healing every kind of disease and illness (Matthew 9:35). However, up until that point, it was only Jesus healing. The need was great, and the people were like sheep without a shepherd. They were confused and helpless. As a result, they prayed to the Lord of the harvest to send workers into His field (Matthew 9:37). Those workers are to work as Jesus did. They are to teach the message of God's Kingdom and to heal every sickness and disease.

In response to the great need, Jesus chose twelve disciples and gave them authority to cast out evil spirits and heal every kind of disease and illness (Matthew 10:1). The ministry increased, and once again Jesus prayed the same prayer—the harvest is plentiful and the workers are few. He asked the Lord of the harvest to send more workers into His fields (Luke 10:2). As a result, Jesus chose seventy-two other disciples and sent them out. He commissioned them to go into all the towns and villages He was planning to visit. He gave them the authority to heal the sick and tell them, *"The kingdom of God has come near"* (Luke 10:10).

After Jesus' resurrection, He commissioned all believers to do the same. The only qualification they must have is to believe.

> *And these signs will accompany those who believe:*
> *In my name they will drive out demons; they will*
> *speak in new tongues; they will pick up snakes with*
> *their hands; and when they drink deadly poison,*
> *it will not hurt them at all; they will place their*
> *hands on sick people, and they will get well* (Mark
> 16:17-18).

These instructions were given after Christ's resurrection. In His death, Jesus satisfied every legal requirement of justice, paying the full price for our sin. He died our death on our behalf and took on Himself the full force of evil. In doing so, He disarmed satan, stripped him of his power, publicly shamed him, triumphing over him by the cross (Colossians 2:15). Jesus reconciled us with the Father. The debt has been paid. Jesus then took back all authority and led the captives who died in faith into God's presence.

On the day of His resurrection, Jesus breathed His Spirit into His disciples and said:

"Peace be with you! As the Father has sent me, I am sending you." And with that he breathed on them and said, "Receive the Holy Spirit. If you forgive anyone's sins, their sins are forgiven; if you do not forgive them, they are not forgiven" (John 20:21).

Just like Jesus was sent from the Father to destroy the works of the devil, so are we sent out with the same mission—to destroy the works of the enemy by healing the sick and casting out evil spirits. God has given us astounding authority and great responsibility. Before His ascension to Heaven, He said:

> *I have been given all authority in heaven and on earth. Therefore, go and make disciples of all the nations, baptizing them in the name of the Father and the Son and the Holy Spirit. Teach these new disciples to obey all the commands I have given you. And be sure of this: I am with you always, even to the end of the age* (Matthew 28:18-20 NLT).

Then Jesus ascended to God's right hand, and with the Father He poured out the Holy Spirit on the church at Pentecost. This made Christ's authoritative headship in the heavens real on earth, through the Body of Christ.

We must exercise this "all authority" that has been given unto us, and if Christ has all authority then satan has none.

The only authority satan has is his influence over people through deception—he is the father of lies (John 8:44). He continues to rule people illegally through sin, sickness, demons, and death, despite the price having been paid by Christ. We need to know that we are the authorized custodians of the earth, enforcing satan's defeat. He has no option but to submit to the authority Christ has given us. We must be aware of his deceptive schemes and crush him underfoot (2 Corinthians 11:14). We carry full authority to destroy the works of the devil as Jesus did, to heal all those who are oppressed by the devil (Acts 10:38). If we don't exercise our authority, we empower satan's illegal rule, and we keep people in their captivity and slavery. We need to be certain that we have full authority over all sickness and all disease. We need to know that authority means delegated power. Policemen who direct traffic during the rush hour just raise their hands and the cars stop. These men don't have the physical power to stop the vehicles if the drivers choose not to stop. But they don't use their own strength to stop traffic; they are strong in the authority that is invested in them by the government they serve. People recognize that authority and stop their cars.

People believe many lies and exclude themselves from using their authority. I used to think that Jesus healed the sick to prove He was God, and therefore I don't need to heal the sick because I am not trying to prove anything. Well, if this argument was correct, then why did the twelve disciples heal the sick, and why did the seventy-two heal the sick, and why would Jesus instruct all believers to heal the sick? Then I ended up believing that this authority was delegated to the church leaders and apostles and not to ordinary individuals. Once again, this was incorrect thinking, because Jesus instructed believers to heal in His name. Our complex minds will find it hard to absorb this, hence the reason Jesus said, *"Let the little children come to me, and do not hinder them, for the kingdom of heaven belongs to such as these"* (Matthew 19:14).

I am reminded of a story of a poor young boy in Africa who lived in the tombs. Every day, people would wrap their dead in cloth and lay them in the graveyard. There was a healing service near this young boy's place. He heard the preacher say that Jesus gave all authority to us, and that all we need to do is believe. The preacher read out Jesus' commission to His disciples: *"Heal the sick, raise the dead, cleanse those who have leprosy, drive out demons. Freely you have received; freely give"* (Matthew 10:8). This young boy liked the idea, and he decided to try it out in the graveyard. Each night, he would walk through the dead bodies and lay his little hands on them and say, "Rise up, in Jesus' name."

To his surprise, some dead bodies started moving and rising up. He was shocked and didn't know what to do. He visited the local church, where the healing service was being held, and told the pastor what had happened. The pastor was shocked also and verified what the young boy was saying. The pastor encouraged the young boy to keep going. The young boy was so excited and continued to do the same each night. Later, the preacher at the healing crusade returned to the village and asked the congregation, "Has anyone prayed for the sick? Has there been anyone casting out demons?" No one lifted their hand. The preacher was discouraged.

The church pastor interrupted the preacher and told him, "I have very encouraging news for you." He asked the young boy to come to the stage and tell what happened.

The young boy boldly climbed up onto the stage and said, "In Jesus' name, I raised many from the dead."

Silence filled the church, and the preacher asked him, "How? What did you do?"

He said, "I did as you said. I simply laid my hands on the freshly dead bodies as they arrived in the graveyard each night and said, 'Get up, in Jesus' name.'" Everyone was in awe of this young boy's faith. This young boy fully believed the Word. He believed that the name of Jesus is higher and stronger than any other name, even death.

So many times we read these same verses but never believe what we read. They end up being head knowledge rather than heart reality. It is time to believe that we have the authority of Christ and that our words carry weight and power. Our words release heaven on earth and can destroy or build the Kingdom.

Chapter 10

THE SECRET BEHIND THE MINISTRY OF JESUS

One of my pursuits in life is to model Jesus in every way—to say what He says and to do what He does. However, in learning from Him we get to see that He healed people differently. At times He gave a command, while at other times He laid His hands on people and healed them. He mixed mud with saliva and put it on a blind man's eyes (John 9:6), while other times sick people begged to touch His cloak and were healed (Matthew 14:36). Jesus didn't model a method or a technique to heal people. He didn't leave us with a manual to follow in order to heal the sick. There must be a secret to the way Jesus ministered. There has to be more than following a formula.

The Gospel of John clearly discloses this secret, showing us that Jesus did what He did, was who He was through the indwelling presence of His Father, by the Holy Spirit's power. This is not a special formula to follow. Skills and methods are important, but the relationship and the intimacy are as essential as the branch abiding in the vine—it can literally do nothing without that abiding (John 15:6). Jesus could do nothing without abiding in the Father by the power of the Holy Spirit (John 14:10), and the Father could do nothing without abiding in the Son by the power of the Holy Spirit. When Philip asked to see the Father, Jesus clearly answered by asking him, *"Don't you believe that I am in the Father, and that the Father is in me?"* (John 14:10). Jesus was in the Father as much as the Father was in Him, and that's what we have been called to experience—total relational oneness with the Father by the power of the Holy Spirit.

Jesus is calling ordinary people to move above and beyond the natural and the normal, to walk with Him in the realm of the miraculous, destroying the work of the devil. He is calling us to love the Father as He loved the Father. Jesus knew His mission; He knew that He was sent by the Father to reveal His love and compassion. This Father destroys the works of the devil through His Son (1 John 3:8). We are invited into the same mission. *"As the Father has sent me, I am sending you"* (John 20:21). At every moment, Jesus was conscious of God as His Father dwelling in Him and operating through Him.

At every moment, He was conscious of the fact that He was working with His Father to free people by destroying evil through healing the sick and casting out demons. Jesus did not wake up one morning and discover who He was. His identity and calling were gradually developed through relationship and intimacy. He loved His Father and practiced His presence, moment by moment, developing a relationship where He began to see what the Father was doing, hear what the Father was saying, and feel what the Father was feeling. By fully trusting in the Father's love, He stepped out to learn and act on what He believed were His Father's thoughts, feelings, and actions. Thus, He increasingly lived, worked, and ministered in union with His loving Father, impacting the world.

In John 5, we meet a lame man who was sick for thirty-eight years. Jesus knew how long this man was sick and healed him. This healing took place on the Sabbath and caused the Pharisees to harass Jesus. Jesus told them, *"My Father is always at his work to this very day, and I too am working"* (John 5:17). The Pharisees tried all the harder to kill Him, because He didn't only break the Sabbath, He called God His Father, thereby *"making himself equal with God"* (John 5:18). So many times, we call God our Father, but we don't fully grasp what that means. It means to be fully backed up by God, and that can only be achieved by acknowledging the Father's love. This was Jesus' greatest secret to success. He said:

For the Father loves the Son and shows him all he does. Yes, and he will show him even greater works than these, so that you will be amazed (John 5:20).

Healing was out of intimacy, out of love for His Father. Jesus continuously relied on the Father to show Him what to do next. He will only do what He sees His Father do (John 5:19). As the love continued, the healing miracles intensified. In John 9, Jesus healed a man who was born blind. Through the Father showing Jesus what to do next, He made mud with saliva and spread the mud over the man's eyes. He asked the man to go and wash in the pool of Siloam, and the man went and washed and came back seeing (John 9:7).

As the intimacy increased, the miracles intensified from healing the sick to raising the dead. In John 11, Jesus raised a man named Lazarus from the dead. This man was dead for four days and the smell was terrible. Mary and Martha struggled to believe, but Jesus revealed to them His secret: *"Did I not tell you that if you believe, you will see the glory of God?"* (John 11:40). He had absolute faith in His Father, who loved Him and was always ready to back Him up. This confidence is displayed in the way Jesus prayed to resurrect Lazarus from the tomb. We don't see Jesus asking His Father, or begging Him, or even reminding Him of how hospitable Lazarus was to Him. He simply displayed absolute faith and trust in the

Father who loved Him. Jesus simply looked up to heaven and said:

> *Father, thank you for hearing me. You always hear me, but I said it out loud for the sake of all these people standing here, so that they will believe you sent me* (John 11:41-42 NLT).

Jesus revealed the key of intimacy to His disciples during His last Passover meal. His last words before He went to the cross explicitly reveal the key of relational intimacy with His Father. He revealed to us that true love requires total obedience and results in intimacy, and intimacy is tied to the revelation of Jesus. He openly said, *"Whoever has my commands and keeps them is the one who loves me. The one who loves me will be loved by my Father, and I too will love them and show myself to them"* (John 14:21). His Father will automatically love the one who loves Jesus, and Jesus will show and manifest Himself through every situation. When we pray for healing, He will manifest Himself; when we cast out devils, He will manifest Himself. But this manifestation starts with being fully in love with Jesus, loving Him for who He is, not because we want Him to do something for us.

I remember meeting my husband at the age of sixteen. We were young and loved each other greatly, despite our differences. My father was overly protective of me, and this caused discomfort because it meant I couldn't see the man I loved as often as I possibly could. I would call him on the phone and express my disappointment with my father. He would say, "Let's try and meet and you can tell me all your problems." When we ended up meeting, somehow we forgot all our problems and just focused on our love. We just loved spending time with each other and continued to fill each other's hearts with our deep love for each other. The love healed every disappointment and hurt. The love was enough and was all we needed. After leaving him, I started to remember that I had forgotten to tell him about my problems. In fact, the problems never bothered me much because I was filled with his love.

The same is true for God. He is our Lover who didn't want heaven without us. He left His glory and honor and humbled Himself to redeem and restore us. He loved us first: *"For God so loved the world"* (John 3:16). Our relationship with Him started with love. Nothing pleases God more than loving Him and literally indulging in His presence. Love Him for who He is and not for what we can get from Him. It is when we delight in the Lord that He gives us the desires of our hearts (Psalm 37:4).

In 1998, I had a huge car accident that left me with severe lower back pain. I learned later that my tailbone was damaged, and, as result, I wasn't able to carry heavy items or bend at all. During the accident, the seat belt locked on my neck, causing pain and damage too. Years went by, and the pain was increasing. One day, I was enjoying God's presence and just indulging in His love. I could feel waves of liquid love just wash over me. I continued to enjoy His love and to focus on how much His love had changed my life. I promised God that I wouldn't ask for anything in prayer. I would just ask for His love to continue flooding and filling me. To my total surprise, I found myself totally and completely healed. I had never prayed specifically to be healed of those conditions, yet His presence brought complete healing to me. I knew that being intimate with Him was key. I wasn't intimate because I wanted something. I was intimate because I realized how much He has loved me.

I was once invited to speak in a meeting, and after preaching I had one lady come up to say hello to me. I gave her a big hug, and she held on to me and embraced me. I felt she just needed love, so I continued hugging her. After that incident, she realized that she was healed from a condition. She was in tears and said to me words I will never forget. She said, "Your love healed me."

I said to her, "You mean His love, through me, healed you."

She said, "Yes, that's what I meant." This opened my eyes to the fact that healing was a product of love and reconciliation with the Father.

The story of Paul and Silas in prison clarifies this truth. Through a vision, the Holy Spirit revealed to Paul that he needed to preach the good news about the

Kingdom in Macedonia. One day, as Paul and Silas were going to the place of prayer, they met a demon-possessed slave girl. She was a fortune-teller who earned a lot of money for her masters. She had a "python spirit," characterizing her as one inspired by Apollo, the god worshiped at Pytho (Delphi). She mockingly said, *"These men are servants of the Most High God, and they have come to tell you how to be saved"* (Acts 16:17 NLT).

This mocking behavior continued day after day until Paul was so exasperated that he cast out the demon from her in Jesus' name, which angered her masters, as they realized that the source of their wealth was now gone. As a result, they dragged Paul and Silas before the authorities and accused them of teaching illegal customs to the Roman citizens. The officials severely beat them and threw them in prison. The jailers were instructed to keep them under maximum security. They put them in the inner dungeon and clamped their feet in the stocks.

Paul and Silas really needed a miracle to take place. They had been severely beaten and must have been in pain. Paul and Silas knew so well how to exercise their authority in Christ. They could have commanded the stocks to break in Jesus' name, or the door to open, or the chains to fall off, repeating the method they used when they were casting out the demon from the slave girl. It worked before, so why not use it again? After all, it was God who led them to come and preach in Macedonia.

The truth is, Paul and Silas didn't have a "one size fits all method," and instead of commanding the stocks to be broken, or the doors to fly off, or the chains to snap, they chose to pray and sing hymns to God (Acts 16:25). They knew that praise brought them into His courts (Psalm 100:4). They were intimate with God, choosing to praise Him in the midst of their pain and trauma. They were not focused on their problems but on His love and power. They didn't need to be set free first in order to praise Him. They praised Him in prison, in the dark small dungeon, with their feet clamped in the stocks. They praised Him in the midst of hurting and bleeding bodies. The other prisoners were listening, perhaps wondering, "How can these people praise their God in such a state?" That's when we learn that intimacy with the Father can and should happen anywhere, even in a prison, or during an illness, or a difficult situation. It is a choice we need to make and a lifestyle we need to abide by.

Suddenly, as they were praising God, a mighty earthquake occurred, shaking the foundations of the prison. All the doors immediately flew open, and the chains of every prisoner fell off. What a mighty deliverance took place. The jailer, seeing the prison doors wide open, assumed the prisoners had escaped and drew his sword to kill himself. Paul assured him that nobody had escaped and everyone was still there. The jailer couldn't get his head around what had actually happened. As a result, he fell down trembling before Paul and Silas, asking them,

"What must I do to be saved?" (Acts 16:30). Paul and Silas lead him to the Lord through asking him to *"believe in the Lord Jesus, and you will be saved"* (Acts 16:31).

The jailer got saved and baptized along with his entire household. The same jailer, who could have been their executioner, took them to his own house to feed them and wash their wounds. What a mighty God we have. His thoughts are not our thoughts, and His ways are not our ways (Isaiah 55:8). How would this jailer have met the Lord, if it wasn't for the presence of Paul and Silas? God is not the one who allows these tough situations we go through. The Bible clearly tells us that we have an enemy who comes to kill, steal, and destroy (John 10:10). However, our God comes to save, heal, and deliver. He uses all situations we go through to bring victory and triumph. That's why we need to rest in Him and choose to be intimate with Him despite anything we go through.

We can only be intimate with God when we no longer fear Him. The fear mentioned in Proverbs 9:10—*"Fear of the Lord is the beginning of wisdom"*—takes place when we love God and choose not to do the wrong thing because of His love for us. But negative fear is when we don't trust God enough and we haven't been perfected in His love. The Bible tells us, *"There is no fear in love. But perfect love drives out fear, because fear has to do with punishment. The one who fears is not made perfect in love. We love because he first loved us"* (1 John 4:18-19).

When we understand this truth, we will be perfected in His love. We will understand that He loved us first, before we made a decision to love Him. His love is perfect at all times. Scientists have found out that love and fear can't coexist at the same time. We are either operating in love or we are operating in fear. Scientists are showing us that there is a massive "unlearning" of negative toxic thoughts when we operate in love. In other words, when we know how much God loves us, we will learn to respond to this love by being intimate with Him. When we operate in love, we cancel fear and melt negative thinking.

John had a special, intimate relationship with Jesus. The Bible clearly tells us he always reclined next to Jesus (John 13:23). Throughout his Gospel, he gives himself a special identity: "the disciple whom Jesus loved." The truth is, Jesus didn't love John more than the other disciples. But John knew he was loved by Jesus and felt that if you would split open Jesus' heart, you would only see John. As a result of this deep, intimate relationship, we see that more was revealed to John than to the others. In John 13, Jesus was deeply troubled, and He told His disciples that one of them would betray Him. The disciples were wondering who this person might be. Simon Peter knew that to get an answer, John would be the one to get it. So, he motioned to John, asking him to find out. That's when we know that intimacy results in getting answers.

Intimacy results in God trusting us with the things most precious to Him. At the time of Jesus' crucifixion, Jesus sees His precious mother Mary standing near the cross with many others, including John, *"the disciple whom he loved."* Jesus looks at His mother and says, *"Woman, here is your son,"* and to John, *"Here is your mother."* From that time on, John took her into his home (John 19:26-27). Intimacy resulted in John being trusted with the precious things, like taking care of Jesus' mother. It is almost like Jesus is telling him, "Now that I am going to My Father, I can trust that you will look after My mother just like Me." How amazing is this!

Intimacy results in deeper revelation. After Jesus' crucifixion, the disciples lost all hope, and they went back to fishing. That night, they didn't catch anything. At dawn, Jesus appeared to them, asking them if they had caught any fish. They didn't know it was Him. Jesus said to them, *"Throw your net on the right side of the boat and you will find some"* (John 21:6). They did, and they couldn't haul in the net because of the amount of fish. With all these clues, they still didn't know that Jesus was in their midst. The only one who knew was the "disciple whom Jesus loved." Intimacy results in revelation.

Intimacy results in long life. The church fathers testify that John outlived the remaining apostles and that he was the only one to die of natural causes. The traditions of most Christian denominations have held that

John the apostle is the author of several Books of the New Testament. What a great revelation—the revelation of love and intimacy with the Father. When we love Him for who He is, His love changes everything. His love heals every organ and every disease. His love breaks prison doors and snaps every chain. It is great to have methods and techniques. But it is even greater to fall in love with our Father and let His genuine, unconditional love heal us and heal others around us.

Chapter 11

HINDRANCES TO HEALING

Seeing someone healed is one of the most joyous sights in this whole world. When someone gets healed from an incurable disease or illness, they feel God's love in action. We can tell people over and over again that God cares about and loves them, but when they get healed this love becomes tangible. They immediately feel God's love and understand that God has compassion for them and that He cares dearly about their life. People start to become intimate with God and believe how real He is. Their test has now become their testimony and they immediately start to share their story with others and spread the good news. Some go back to their doctors and share what took place. They come back and tell us that, "My doctor was surprised and said there is no other explanation for this other than it must be the hand of

God," while others take it to their workplace or their families and share what God did to them. They become so encouraged to pray for others, and they feel like telling the whole world that God is so real and, "What God did with me, He is able to do to you."

In other words, seeing people receive their healing is glorious and uplifting. It is really when heaven touches earth and when the glory of God is revealed to us. Healing is His presence and His essence. However, what happens when people get prayed for fervently, and they don't get healed and die? Early on in the ministry, I remembered Dr. Randy Clark telling us important keys to keep going in the healing ministry. The key was that we don't take the glory when someone gets healed, and we don't take the blame.

In Acts 3, when Peter and John healed a man who was lame from birth, the people were absolutely astounded at what had just happened. But Peter didn't take any glory to himself; rather, he used the miracle to point the people straight to God. He said to the people, *"Why do you stare at us as if by our own power or godliness we had made this man walk? The God of Abraham, Isaac and Jacob, the God of our fathers, has glorified his servant Jesus"* (Acts 3:12-13). As a result of this healing, many people believed in God, and the number of believers now totaled 5,000 (Acts 4:4). This is a great example of Peter not taking the glory and giving all glory to God. He acknowledged that this healing couldn't have been made possible by his power or his godliness. It wasn't even because he was prayed up and on fire for God, for the Book of Acts tell us that they were about to enter the temple to take part in the three o'clock prayer service (Acts 3:1). They fully acknowledged that this miracle was to glorify the name of the Lord Jesus and to bring people to faith in Him. In fact, a miracle that doesn't connect people to God is absolutely useless. Therefore, the concept of not taking the glory is essential in order to allow the healing miracle to connect people to God.

However, the hard one is "not taking the blame." This is the main reason why so many quit praying for others. They have prayed for people and not seen anything happen. Once we learn this very important key, we will keep going despite all disappointment. I once heard a great German evangelist share his heart about this topic. He revealed an amazing key which kept us going. He said, "If you are praying for one hundred people and the first ninety-nine don't get healed, then pray for the last one with the attitude that all the previous ninety-nine were healed." We need to elevate the Word of God above our personal experiences. The Word of God is our final authority. Our experiences must be judged by Scripture, not Scripture by our experiences.

I remember early in the ministry we held a healing service, and it was a glorious meeting. The hall was full, we needed to bring extra chairs to seat the people, and the worship was powerful. It felt like an open heaven. After the preaching of the word, we started to give out words of knowledge and then asked those who needed prayer to come to the front. After praying for everyone, we then asked if they could test themselves and check if they were healed. Some people were excited and in tears and testified to their healing, while others went back to their seats feeling God didn't want to heal them. My heart was broken, especially because I knew how much they needed to get healed. After the meeting, our ministry team was equally distressed and raised their concerns. They started telling us that it is not fair that God didn't heal those people. Others said that we shouldn't pray for people corporately, so that those who don't get healed don't distance themselves from God. We could see the disappointment in their eyes. Some started to blame themselves and said, "Maybe God didn't call us to heal the sick," or "Maybe I need to fast more or pray more." Others kept saying, "Maybe God is trying to teach those people something through their sickness, or maybe it is not His will to heal at all times," while others kept asking, "Why, God? Why, God? Why, God?"

I remember going into my prayer closet and literally beating myself. I was upset at God, and I said, "I kept saying, 'Be healed in Jesus' name' and nothing happened. Why, God, did You not come through? Please answer me and tell me—what have I done wrong?" I kept telling

God, "If Jesus was physically present in tonight's service, then You would have healed them all. Lord, I believe that through Your Holy Spirit, You are in us, so why, Lord?" Because I was so sad, I couldn't really hear God say anything other than just feeling the Holy Spirit comfort me and embrace me. I felt that the Holy Spirit took out of me all the pain I was carrying and healed my broken heart. I couldn't understand fully what was happening, but I felt that God said, "If you continue and do not stop, I will show you the keys to heal people. When you keep going, you are declaring that you trust Me more than your personal experience." I felt God say, "I want you to keep going deeper and to keep growing in Me, for you lack nothing." God showed me a beautiful verse in His Word, and it says that I have been made complete through my union with Christ, who is head over every ruler and authority (Colossians 2:10).

My spirit loved this verse, yet my intellect could not really understand it. I held on to it until someone explained it to me. It is like when a mother gives birth to a newborn baby. First the nurse checks every part of the newborn baby. The nurse will check that the baby can hear, can see, and that the heart is working. Once all the checks are done, we have a complete baby. However, this baby can't walk, can't talk, and can't see well. All the organs are there; however, the baby hasn't developed yet. The baby has as many muscles as a bodybuilder, but they are not developed yet. The more the baby grows and develops, the more the baby is able to see, walk, and talk. This key is really what kept me going. I knew that I had been made complete through my union with Christ and that I had lots of growing up to do.

To start this process, I started to study the Word over again, looking out to see if Jesus faced hindrances to His ministry. In Mark 6, we see Jesus returning to His hometown in Nazareth:

> *The next Sabbath, he began teaching in the synagogue, and many who heard him were amazed. They asked, "Where did he get all this wisdom and the power to perform such miracles?" Then they scoffed, "He's just a carpenter, the son of Mary and the brother of James, Joseph, Judas, and Simon. And his sisters live right here among us." They were deeply offended and refused to believe in him. Then Jesus told them, "A prophet is honored everywhere except in his own hometown and among his relatives and his own family." And because of their unbelief, he couldn't do any miracles among them except to place his hands on a few sick people and heal them. And he was amazed at their unbelief* (Mark 6:2-6 NLT).

To say that Jesus, *the Son of God* to whom God gave *the Spirit with no limit,* "couldn't do any miracles" is a big statement, and the cause behind this hindrance was *unbelief.* The people were familiar with Jesus, as they were from His hometown, and, as a result, they scoffed at Him. That's when familiarity breeds contempt. When people are familiar with you and they know that you are the normal ordinary Christian and now you are healing the sick and raising the dead, they will be full of unbelief. Unbelief is a massive hindrance to healing. The only thing that would melt away unbelief is faith. We know that faith comes by hearing, and hearing by the Word of God (Romans 10:17). Smith Wigglesworth, whom God used in a mighty way in the area of divine healing, believed that healing came through faith. He knew that faith comes by hearing, so he would read the Word of God out loud to himself so that he could hear the Word and boost his faith. People come for prayer filled with baggage, and their baggage, such as unbelief, can hinder their divine healing.

This is a great principle, but it can't be used as a rule because even in Nazareth, where they were full of unbelief, Jesus did heal some. Sometimes when we know there is so much unbelief, we cease to pray for healing because we can see the unbelief. Jesus, who is our great teacher, knew that they were full of unbelief, and yet He prayed for their healing. Unbelief can be a hindrance; however, God is sovereign.

Another great hindrance to divine healing is the traditions people create and end up believing. In Mark 7, we see Jesus rebuking the Pharisees for creating many made-up traditions. Jesus says to them, *"You cancel the word of God in order to hand down your own tradition"* (Mark 7:13 NLT).

THE TRADITION OF HAVING GREAT FAITH

One of the made-up traditions is that of faith. There is the belief that you need to have great faith in order to be healed. The truth is, God looks for faith, and the Bible tells us that without faith it is impossible to please God (Hebrews 11:6). Many times in the gospels we see sick people move in great faith and receive their healing. A great example is that woman with the issue of blood in the Bible. She was suffering for twelve years with constant bleeding. She had gone to many doctors and spent all the money she had with no success. When she heard about Jesus, she came up behind Him and touched His robe, for she thought to herself, *"If I can just touch his robe, I will be healed"* (Mark 5:28 NLT).

This was a radical act of faith. Women in those days were not meant to be in the midst of men, especially a bleeding woman who was considered defiled and ceremonially unclean. Despite all those challenges, we see this woman move in great faith, and, as a result, her bleeding stopped and she could feel in her body that she had been healed of her terrible condition (Mark 5:29). Jesus did not rebuke her for touching Him while bleeding; in fact, He publicly commended her by saying, *"Your faith has healed you"* (Matthew 9:22).

Another great example is that of the two blind men who followed Jesus and were shouting, *"Son of David, have mercy on us!"* Jesus asked them, *"Do you believe I can make you see?"* They replied, *"We do."* Then He touched their eyes and said, *"Because of your faith, it will happen"* (Matthew 9:27-29 NLT). Here we see that the principle of faith is important, but once we make a tradition out of it and turn it into a law, then we hinder what God is able to do in our lives. A great example of this is the man in Mark 9 whose son was possessed with an evil spirit. He brought his son to Jesus' disciples and they were unable to heal him. This man didn't have much faith and said to Jesus, *"If you can do anything, take pity on us and help us."* Jesus replied, *"Everything is possible for one who believes."* The man exclaimed, *"I do believe; help me overcome my unbelief!"* (Mark 9:22-24). Jesus commanded the spirit to get out of the boy and never enter him again, and the boy was healed.

So many times, we create a tradition that tells people that unless they have great faith, they will not be healed. As a result, we create a wall and start to believe that we don't have great faith, and therefore we won't get healed. This creates a hindrance in our hearts. The story of the four friends who lowered their sick friend on a mat and placed him right in front of Jesus is another great example. The sick man didn't have faith, but his friends had faith for him, and Jesus healed him. The principal issue of faith is very important, but once we make a tradition out of it then we create a hindrance. God is much bigger than our faith, and what we don't know about God is much more than what we do know.

The tradition of sin in someone's life can greatly hinder healing. Some people come for prayer, and when they don't get healed they get told that it is because they might have sin in their life. Sin can definitely be an open door or a root cause for sickness or infirmity. In Mark 2, some men brought a paralyzed man to Jesus through the roof. The cause of this man's paralysis was his sin. At first, Jesus said to the man, *"Son, your sins are forgiven"* (Mark 2:5). When the teachers of the law heard Him, they said He was blaspheming. But Jesus proved to them that this man's sins were really forgiven, telling him, *"Get up, take your mat and go home"* (Mark 2:11). The physical healing was a perfect proof that his sin was forgiven. Jesus forgave the sin first, then healed the man.

However, in John 5 we meet a lame man who had been lame for thirty-eight years. This man also had sin in his life. Jesus physically healed him, and later He said to him, *"See, you are well again. Stop sinning or something worse may happen to you"* (John 5:14). In this case, the sin in this man's life didn't stop Jesus from healing him. Jesus dealt with the sin issue later, but his sin didn't hinder Jesus from healing. We are called to be holy, as God is holy (1 Peter 1:16). Jesus constantly asked people to repent, for the Kingdom of God was at hand (Mark 1:15). The apostle Paul told both Jews and Greeks that they must turn to God in repentance and have faith in our Lord Jesus. After Pentecost, Peter addressed the people, telling them to *"Repent, then, and turn to God, so that your sins may be wiped out, that times of refreshing may come from the Lord"* (Acts 3:19). Therefore, it is important we repent from sin and turn to God. However, we can't turn that into a tradition or a law. When people don't get healed, we should not tell them, "It is because you have sin in your life, and once you repent then God will heal you."

The same is true for salvation; God didn't wait until we clean ourselves up and then come to save us. The Bible tells us that while we were sinners, Christ died for us (Romans 5:8). The same applies to divine healing; Christ has already paid the price for us to be healed. Our job is to heal the sick, not analyze their situation and play God.

God taught us this concept practically. On one occasion while we were gathered for prayer, two gay men came into the hall and sat next to each other. It was the first time we had ever seen them, and it was obvious that they were together. At the end of the meeting, we invited everyone needing prayer to come to the front and get prayed for. To our surprise, the two gay men came to the front. We asked them what they needed prayer for. One of them said, "I had an accident and I have excruciating back pain."

I found it extremely hard to pray, and while I seemed nice on the outside, I was very judgmental on the inside. I was thinking, "How can God heal you? There is no way. You need to repent first, then I will attempt praying for your healing."

While having all these background thoughts, we started to pray. To our shock and surprise, the man started shouting and saying, "I got healed! Jesus healed me!"

We were shocked and confused. I wanted to ask God, "How did You heal such a sinner?" What happened next shocked me. The man who had just got healed knelt on the floor, confessing his sins, and asked God to forgive him. It was only then that we understood Romans 2:4, which tells us that His kindness leads to repentance. They felt God's kindness toward them, and they couldn't help but repent and come back to the Lord.

This experience taught me not to judge and, more importantly, not to quickly come up with answers when healing doesn't happen. Sometimes the best answer is, "I don't know why this person wasn't healed." This is a very humbling answer and it is better than making up doctrines to justify why this person wasn't healed. I need to constantly remind myself of my role. My role is to pray, and God's will is to heal. It is very important not to hurt people with our healing ministry and tell people, "You didn't get healed because you don't have enough faith, or because you have sin in your life." Jesus never hurt people with His healing ministry. He simply healed all who came to Him and had compassion for people. We need to imitate Christ in every way and reveal His love to a hurting world. We are called to live in holiness, but God is much bigger than our sin and His love covers a multitude of sins. Let's have the mind of Christ and seek to go deeper in God instead of making traditions that hinder the healing.

Chapter 12

SPIRIT, SOUL, AND BODY

Understanding the relationship between spirit, soul, and body is crucial to receiving your healing. First Thessalonians 5:23, tells us, *"May God himself, the God of peace, sanctify you through and through. May your whole spirit, soul and body be kept blameless at the coming of our Lord Jesus Christ."* Even though God's Word teaches us that we are a three-part being, very few people practice a functional understanding of that concept. Most people acknowledge a physical part and an emotional, mental, inner part.

Our body is obvious. It is the physical part of us, which houses the spirit and the soul. It is the part we see in a mirror. We are constantly in touch with our bodies. Our body can tell us how it feels. It can tell us if we are having back pain, or a headache, or we are coming down with flu.

Our soul includes our mind, will, emotions, and conscience. We are constantly in touch with our soul. If you were talking to me face to face, you'd be seeing my body, but you would be speaking to my soul.

We can feel both our bodies and our soul. If someone touches my shoulder, I instantly feel that. If someone spoke hurtful words to me, it would hurt my soul. We are constantly in touch with our bodies and our soul. That's not the case with our spirit. Jesus shared a fundamental truth when He was speaking to Nicodemus. He said, *"That which is born of the flesh is flesh, and that which is born of the Spirit is spirit"* (John 3:6 NKJV). Jesus meant there is no direct access between the spirit and the body. They are interrelated, as we will see later, but spirit is spirit and flesh is flesh. You can simply draw a clear-cut demarcation between your spirit and your emotions, and both should not be mixed together. Here we find one of the greatest problems in Christian life.

If you don't understand that spiritual realities can't be felt, then you will be confused when God's Word says that by His stripes you have been healed (1 Peter 2:24). You will be confused when God's Word declares that *"The Spirit of him who raised Jesus from the dead is living in you"* (Romans 8:11). You will be confused when you read that you have the same power that raised Jesus from the dead (Ephesians 1:18-20). If you think truth can be discerned through your natural senses, then you will be confused when the Bible says that you are a brand-new creation who can do the same work as Jesus did (2 Corinthians 5:17; John 14:12).

Without understanding the spirit, soul, and body, you will look at your sick body and wonder—where is that power? You will think, "I don't really have this power," or "I don't really believe the Bible says I do."

UNDERSTANDING THE SPIRIT REALM

Because we have no natural way to see or feel our spirit, the only way to perceive spiritual truth is through the Bible. Simply take God's Word and believe it. Jesus said, *"The Spirit gives life; the flesh counts for nothing. The words I have spoken to you—they are full of the Spirit and life"* (John 6:63). Here comes a very important key. If you want to know what your spirit is like, you must find out from the Word of God. We can't go by how we feel, see, or perceive. God's Word is spirit and life.

When you get born again, your spirit becomes instantly perfect. God's Word reflects who you are in the spirit. It is like looking in a mirror to check your makeup. You have never seen your face. Your eyes never see your face. You see your face in a reflection, and you believe what you see. If you want to check your makeup, you don't go by how you feel because you can't feel your make-up. You simply go to the mirror and trust what you see.

The same is true for your spirit. When you read the Word, you are seeing a reflection of your spirit. You get to know that your spirit has been forgiven, healed, and set free. You get to know that you are a new creation, and the same mighty power that raised Christ from the dead lives inside of you. The Bible tells us that every born-again believer has undergone a complete transformation. *"Therefore, if anyone is in Christ, the new creation has come: The old has gone, the new is here!"* (2 Corinthians 5:17). God's Word tells us that every born-again believer, by His stripes, was healed (1 Peter 2:24). Both these verses are past tense—something that already took place in our spirit. Our spirit is now brand new and totally healed.

Unless we understand the spirit, soul, and body, we will be set up for confusion. After reading these verses, we look at our sick body and notice that we are still sick. In my body, old things have not gone, and new things have not come. For example, if I was overweight before I got saved, I will still be overweight after I get saved. The same is true for our soul. Your soul wasn't the part of you that completely changed. For example, if you didn't know science before you got saved, you won't know science after you get saved. If you were depressed before you got saved, you will stay depressed until you change the way your soul thinks by believing God's Word.

Your soul can be transformed now to the degree you renew your mind, change your attitudes, and conform your values to the Word of God. This is a process, and it doesn't happen automatically.

Release What You've Already Got

Jesus fully redeemed us on the cross. But we must reclaim what Christ paid for.

At salvation, your spirit has totally changed. Your body and soul have been impacted by what happened, but the change is not total or complete.

People who don't understand this reality will be greatly disappointed. They say, "I thought I was healed." Then unbelief kicks in, and many doubt God's promises because they are using their natural senses and don't understand that there is no direct access to their spirit.

The truth is, your spirit has totally changed. You are not in the process of getting a new spirit. Everything you will ever need in your Christian life is already present in its entirety in your spirit. At this moment, your born-again spirit is healed, perfect, and complete. You won't get a new spirit when you get to Heaven, nor will your spirit need to mature. Your born-again spirit is as pure as Jesus is.

The Pivot Point

After being born again, the rest of our Christian walk is simply renewing and releasing. As we renew our mind and believe God's Word, our soul will agree with what's already transpired in our spirit. When our soul comes into alignment with what it sees in God's Word, what's already in your spirit (healing) releases into your soul and body. That's how many get healed when they renew their mind.

If your spirit and soul agree, that's two parts against one. The majority rule, so your soul and body will experience the healing, life, and power that are already present in your spirit. On the other hand, when your soul agrees with your body (majority rules again) and is dominated by the natural realms, then the flow of healing, life, and power stops. What's in your spirit must flow through your soul in order to get out to your body.

Spirit   Soul   Body

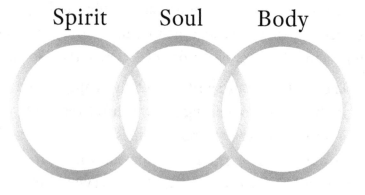

Consider the following diagram of three circles inside each other. The outer circle is your body. It is the part of you that you can see and feel. Then you have an inner part that can't be seen, but can be felt. That's your soul. Notice how the soul touches both the spirit and the body.

Most people don't realize that their spirit is their core, their inner being. They primarily function out of a soulish realm, believing what they think and feel is the reality. They might perceive their soul as their core, not their spirit.

Because your life comes from your spirit, it is the innermost circle of the three. Notice how your spirit is completely surrounded by your soul. It has no direct access to your body. That's why everything that comes out from your spirit to your body must go through your mental, emotional part.

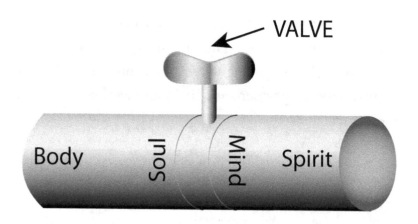

With the pipe diagram, one side represents your spirit and the other your body. Your soul acts as a valve in between the two. When you open the valve, what's in your spirit can flow through to your body. Depending on how open it is, the flow of life (healing) can be a trickle, a small stream, or rivers (John 7:37). When the valve is closed, the flow of life (healing) from spirit to body shuts off. Remember that in your spirit you have the same power that raised Jesus from the dead (Ephesians 1:18-20). Yet it is possible to have this power and never manifest it. Without opening the valve by renewing your mind to God's Word, the healing in your spirit won't be able to reach your sick body. All the resurrection life just stays shut inside until we change our mind.

You could actually die with all this power that raised Jesus from the dead sitting untapped within you. It would be like dying from thirst while leaning against a well full of life-giving water. If you are dominated by what you feel, your soul is agreeing with your body against your spirit. You say, "I feel sick and my body hurts. The doctor said I don't have long to live. Here is the doctor's report to prove it." Even though you have the resurrection life of God in your spirit, you can shut it off so that not one drop of life-giving power can ever touch your physical body.

You can experience anxiety, anger, and depression, all while possessing God's love, peace, and joy in your spirit (Galatians 5:22). Your body doesn't really control anything. It just goes with the flow of what it sees, tastes, hears, smells, and feels, unless otherwise influenced by the soul. When your soul agrees with your spirit, the life of God in you will manifest in your physical body. You will experience healing and deliverance.

Here we recognize that the Christian life isn't a process of "getting from God." Instead, it is a process of renewing my mind and learning to release what I've already received. It is much easier to release something I have already got than to go get something I don't yet have!

My firsthand experience of this principle really helped me understand this powerful concept. I was ministering to two lovely women who were both diagnosed with stage four cancer. The first woman, called Angela, came from the Coptic Orthodox church. Unfortunately, many in this church believe ungodly traditions. Some call cancer "the sickness of the kingdom." The reason they give it that name is that when people get diagnosed with this disease, they start thinking more of death and going to heaven. They start to get themselves right with God and get closer to Him. They believe that when God is ready to take you to heaven, He inflicts cancer on you to get you ready.

Angela grew up in this environment. She fell in love with a young man who became disappointed with God and turned atheist. During their engagement, Angela was diagnosed with this terrible disease. She heard of our healing ministry and decided to come alone. As we were praying for her, we felt that she wasn't receiving our prayers and seemed confused. As we prayed for her, she kept repeating, "Only if it is Your will, God." We tried to explain to Angela that God's will is to heal her and make her well. But she found it hard to believe us because every Sunday she went to church to have communion, and she was being assured that God had given her a gift called "the disease of the kingdom" and she didn't want to lose her gift. I tried hard to explain to Angela that her spirit was full of resurrection power and that her soul (mind) was trapping that power because it was not renewed. Angela found it hard to believe me. Unfortunately, she didn't read the Bible or renew her mind to receive her inheritance.

Sadly, I was called to pray for Angela on her death-bed. I walked in as she was dying. Her face looked pale, and she was gasping for air. Her husband was standing there watching me. I looked in her eyes and said, "Angela, Jesus paid the price for your healing."

She looked at me and said, "Let His will be done."

With tears in my eyes, I said to her, "Angela, it is His will to heal you." At that moment, I hardly got an answer. I started praying and rebuking cancer with tears in my eyes. I commanded cancer to shrivel and die in Jesus' name. But sadly, Angela did die and went to be with the Lord. I am not saying that I can fully explain why Angela wasn't healed. Only God knows that answer. All I am saying is that up until her final moments, she refused to change her mind and believe that her healing was fully paid for, that in her spirit she had the same power that raised Jesus from the dead, and she was already healed in her spirit. She needed to renew her mind so that the resurrection power, which was in her spirit, would reach her sick body.

On the other side, I was ministering to a different person named Mary. She was also diagnosed with stage four breast cancer. She was given less than three months to live. Mary was a believer, but used to be against those who pray for healing. To her, physical healing was not important. The most important thing was spiritual healing and assurance of going to heaven. Mary had three sisters who all died from the same type of breast cancer in the lymph nodes. Mary knew there was a calling on her life, and she now really appreciates the healing ministry. However, she held on to many false beliefs about healing. She was certain that she was going to die because all her sisters had died from the same disease. She had gone through a tough time in her life and lived in sin for some time. She really hated her sin and used to walk around her house saying, "I wish I would get cancer and die. I don't want to live." Mary continued to say those same words each day until she noticed a big lump growing between her neck and her shoulder. Mary believed that her cancer could either be God punishing her for her sin or a generational family curse from the bloodline. Mary felt dirty and unworthy to be healed.

When we started ministering to her, we knew that her mind needed to be renewed and that she needed to understand the condition of her spirit. When she understood that her spirit was pure and clean, she understood that the spirit of Him who raised Jesus from the dead was living in her, and that by Jesus' stripes she was healed. However, due to the poor condition of her soul, the power that was in her spirit was trapped. We explained to her the importance of repentance and reminded her that if we confess our sins, He is faithful and just and will forgive us our sins and purify us from all unrighteousness (1 John 1:9). We explained to her the nature of God. God is a healer who heals. He doesn't punish us with sickness if we sin. In fact, He paid the price of all our sins and all our sickness. Mary was listening and absorbing all we said. We had many sessions together.

On one occasion, she mentioned that there was no way she could be healed because all her sisters died from the exact same thing. At that point, we needed to explain generational curses and break them. We explained the meaning of the following verse.

> *The Lord is slow to anger, abounding in love and forgiving sin and rebellion. Yet he does not leave the guilty unpunished; he punishes the children for the sin of the parents to the third and fourth generation* (Numbers 14:18).

We repented for the sins of the parents unto the fourth generation and broke all generational curses in Jesus' name. We declared that the blood of Jesus would stand as a wall of separation between Mary and all previous generations.

As we continued to minister to her, her test results were getting better and better. She stuck John 11:4 on her mirror: "*This sickness will not end in death. No, it is for God's glory so that God's Son may be glorified through it.*" She started to believe that God wasn't punishing her and that she didn't need to die like her sisters because every generational curse had been broken and she belonged to a royal lineage. As her thinking started to change, she became more and more convinced that God was on her side and that He wanted her healed.

Our next challenge was her thinking that she was not worthy of this healing because she deserved cancer. We started to explain to her, that just like no one deserves God's salvation, no one deserves God's healing. That healing is a work of grace and we simply need to receive it by faith. All these sessions transformed Mary's thinking and enabled her soul (mind) to be in alignment with her spirit. She dedicated time to study the Word and hold on to every promise.

Mary's condition started to get better and better. Doctors couldn't find a medical explanation for her improvement. Years went by, and while her cancer didn't totally disappear, she is alive and well. She still believes in her total healing and fully trusts the Lord. She has stopped asking God to heal her, and realized that He has already given her everything in her spirit. Her journey now is renewing her mind and releasing the power in her spirit to touch her sick body.

Once we understand this powerful truth, everything will change. It is not a guarantee that once you believe you will automatically get healed. But just like evangelism, the more we evangelize, the more people respond. The more we unpack the truth about healing, the more likely we are to get healed.

Chapter 13

THE PRINCIPLE OF FAITH

F aith is one of the most critical key factors in receiving and ministering healing. In order to be effective
ministers, we must understand faith and how it operates
in the healing process. Many believers don't understand
this principle and get more confused researching it. Some
will say, "I don't have enough faith," and their whole life
pursuit will become about fasting for more faith, praying
for more faith, asking God for more faith, running from
conference to conference to try and get more faith. As a
result, I decided to study the topic in depth and continued to seek the Holy Spirit for revelation about this topic.
The truth He revealed shook me and set me free from so
much doubt and confusion.

As I studied His word, the following quotes were mentioned about faith.

- There is *"lack of faith"* that resists God's healing (Mark 6:1-6).

- There is *"little faith"* that is rebuked and fails to receive God's miracles (Matthew 8:26; 17:20).

- There is *"wavering faith"* that is challenged and strengthened for healing (Mark 5:35-36).

- There is *"faith as small as a mustard seed"* that can move mountains (Matthew 17:20).

- There is *"measure of faith"* that we all receive and must put to use (Romans 12:3).

- There is *"great faith"* based on confidence in God's authority and power (Matthew 8:10; 15:28).

- There is the *"gift of faith"*—an impartation of God's faith that works miracles despite all opposition (1 Corinthians 12:9).

This caused even more confusion on the topic, because I really wanted to make sure that I had *great faith*. I needed to know how to operate in *great faith*, thinking that if I was able to operate in *great faith* then I would definitely see many mighty miracles like those great men and woman of God who were referred to as the "generals of faith." As a result, my search for the biblical definition of faith began with a focus on finding out the main ingredient that constitutes *great faith.*

WHAT IS FAITH?

The Bible tells us that faith is confidence in what we hope for and assurance about what we do not see (Hebrews 11:1). Therefore, biblical faith is belief, reliance, confidence, and trust in God. It is not faith in concepts or things, such as ideologies, doctrines, or people. It is confidence in God Himself. This confidence develops out of relational intimacy with a loving and compassionate God. It is a confidence that is birthed from knowing God for who He is, and the more I know Him the more confident I become and the more I become assured that what I am hoping for will happen. Therefore, faith is relational, not a formula based on laws. It is not a manipulative mechanism or a magical power to get God to do things for us. When used in that way, it's not faith but witchcraft. Therefore, faith in the power of positive thinking, in a formula, in a religious ritual, in a person, or even in faith itself is all idolatry.

Real biblical faith is a powerful mystery because it is based on our relationship with and trust in God. This trust generates faith and causes God to move. Many times when we hear of Jesus being moved by faith, it's because He understood that a person's act of faith (like touching the hem of His garment) was an outward demonstration of internal trust in His nature, character, will, and ability. The act of faith was based on something bigger that was happening on the inside. Thus, we are told, *"without faith it is impossible to please God, because anyone who comes to him must believe that he exists and that he rewards those who earnestly seek him"* (Hebrews 11:6). One can't seek Him without having a relationship with Him. Through relationship, we get to know and be sure that God exists and that He cares and rewards those who seek Him. Therefore, the foundation of confidence and trust is relationship, and the stronger the relationship the greater the confidence and the trust in asking God and receiving abundantly.

GREAT FAITH

Jesus only commended two people's faith as being great, neither of whom were in covenant with God. The first was a Roman centurion, who had a paralyzed servant who was in great suffering (Matthew 8:5-7). Although he was a Gentile and was not in covenant with the God of Israel, he bypassed all obstacles and hindrances. He stepped out and asked Jesus to heal his servant. Jesus agreed, and even offered to go to his home and heal his servant. Interestingly, this man's response amazed Jesus. He replied by saying:

> *Lord, I do not deserve to have you come under my roof. But just say the word, and my servant will be healed. **For I myself am a man under authority,** with soldiers under me. I tell this one, "Go," and he goes; and that one, "Come," and he comes. I say to my servant, "Do this," and he does it* (Matthew 8:8-9).

This man's faith was truly amazing. Although he was not in covenant with God, he understood two amazing revelations. First, he understood how authority operates. This is a concept many believers struggle with today.

At this time in history, Israel was ruled by the Roman Empire. Although this Roman centurion was living in Israel, he knew that he was representing Rome and carried the authority of the Roman emperor. He understood that, when his soldiers saw him, they saw Caesar in Rome. He understood that when he gave out orders, they must be followed because it was not him giving out those orders, it was Caesar in Rome. He understood that to operate under the name of the Roman emperor was to operate in the same authority.

Second, the centurion applied the way he understood authority to the way Jesus operated. He understood that Jesus was operating under heavenly authority and that when He released a command, that command must be executed because His heavenly Father would back it up.

The teachers of the religious law found it hard to understand this concept. In actual fact, they wanted to kill Jesus for healing a lame man on the Sabbath. Jesus gave them this answer: *"Very truly I tell you, the Son can do nothing by himself; he can do only what he sees his Father doing, because whatever the Father does the Son also does"* (John 5:19). In other words, the Son is fully under the authority of His Father. Therefore, the Roman centurion understood that Jesus was under His Father's authority and that there was no need for Jesus to be physically present, because the word was backed up by His Father and would definitely be executed. The Bible tells us that when Jesus heard this, He marveled and said to those following Him, *"Truly I tell you, I have not found anyone in Israel with such great faith"* (Matthew 8:10). And He said to him, *"'Go! Let it be done just as you believed it would.' And his servant was healed at that moment"* (Matthew 8:13). It was truly amazing to have this level of faith despite not having a covenant with God.

The other person who was commended for having great faith was the Canaanite woman who approached Jesus Christ to heal her demon-possessed daughter.

Being a Gentile meant that she was not in covenant with the God of Israel and had absolutely no right to ask. Despite all obstacles, she came to Jesus, crying out and saying, *"Lord, Son of David, have mercy on me! My daughter is demon-possessed and suffering terribly"* (Matthew 15:22). In her cry for mercy, she called Him "Lord," recognizing His lordship over everything including demons, and "Son of David" recognizing Him as the Messiah. Despite her plea for help, Jesus kept silent, and His disciples urged Him to send her away because she bothered them (Matthew 15:23). At that, Jesus moved her away by telling her, *"I was sent only to the lost sheep of Israel"* (Matthew 15:24).

The woman came and knelt before Jesus and begged for His healing. What is perplexing is Jesus' seemingly cold remark to the woman. He said to her, *"It is not right to take the children's bread and toss it to the dogs"* (Matthew 15:25-26). This was a direct reference to her not being in covenant relationship with God. But instead of getting offended, the woman admitted that she was a dog that eats the crumbs that fall from their master's table. And hearing her response Jesus said to her, *"'Woman, you have great faith! Your request is granted.' And her daughter was healed at that moment"* (Matthew 15:28).

It's quite obvious that the only two people who were ever told by Jesus that they have "great faith" were two people who were not covenant people. They had no covenant with God; therefore, it was truly amazing that they had the faith to ask God (Jesus) for anything. They had no right to ask. When you have no right to ask, it takes great faith to ask. In fact, Jesus rebuked His disciples because they didn't display the same degree of confidence in God (Jesus) as these two "heathen" people, despite being in covenant relationship with God.

To simplify what I am saying, let me give this demonstration. If my earthly father has invited a stranger for dinner and I walk into the dining room with a request, would it be easier to ask my father or the stranger? Of course, it would be my father whom I know and have a relationship with. I would require so much more faith to ask the stranger because I don't know them, and much less faith to ask my father because I know him. This truth is powerful, because relationship is the foundation of faith, and the stronger the relationship the stronger the faith. Nowhere in the New Testament after Jesus' death and resurrection are Christians told to "have faith." Christians don't have a faith problem. We have faith or we are not born again.

OUR INHERITANCE

Every born-again Christian already has the same quality and quantity of faith that Jesus has. Isn't that awesome!

In Ephesians 2:8, Paul says, *"For it is by grace you have been saved, through faith—and this is not from yourselves, it is the gift of God."* It's God's grace that saves us, but not His grace alone. If that were so, then everyone would be saved because God's grace has come to all men (Titus 2:11).

We have to put faith in God's grace, but the faith that we use isn't our own human faith. This verse says that faith is the gift of God.

The same measure of faith we need for salvation is the same measure of faith we need for healing. It doesn't take more faith to heal the sick than to get saved.

We don't need to ask God to give us more faith, because He has already given us Christ and in Him we have been blessed with every spiritual blessing in the heavenly realms (Ephesians 1:3), and that includes faith. Through union with His Holy Spirit, we received the spirit of adoption, not slavery, enabling us to call Him *"Abba, Father"* (Romans 8:15). In actual fact, through our union with Christ we have received an inheritance from God (Ephesians 1:11).

This inheritance makes healing our right. Not out of entitlement but out of union and relationship with God. That explains Jesus' statement to the Canaanite woman when He told her, *"It is not right to take the children's bread and toss it to the dogs"* (Matthew 15:25-26). In other words, healing and deliverance is the children's bread. It's their inheritance and can only be received through Jesus, because *"I am the bread of life"* (John 6:48). This indicates that through our union with Christ, we have an inheritance, which was already given to us. Our healing has already been given to us, and we don't need great faith to ask God to do what He has already done.

As Christians we already have faith and healing. We received it when we received Jesus. Our job is to drive out the enemy of God who tries to keep us from walking in our healing. Once we evict the outlaw called sickness or disease, we live in divine health, which God has provided through the death and resurrection of Jesus. We were healed when we got saved; now we must drive out the enemy that's living illegally in God's property.

THE TRUTH ABOUT FAITH

Every born-again believer already has faith. Therefore, *"Everything is possible for one who believes"* (Mark 9:23). That's because of who God is and not because of our faith. Faith involves knowledge and expectation. People came to Jesus for His healing as they heard of His compassion and power to heal. *"Faith comes from hearing... the word of God"* (Romans 10:17 NKJV). That doesn't mean that the more you hear, the more you have faith. It means that as you hear the word, the faith you already have is activated.

God doesn't disappoint; He acts on behalf of His children—even when He does not act or intervene when we expect. In that case, a deeper test of faith is at work, teaching us to be faithful to God beyond our understanding and expectation, beyond healing or no healing. This

The Principle of Faith

does not mean easy acceptance if faith is not apparently answered, but rather perseverance in faith by persistent request until God does something.

Jesus taught this principle in Luke 11:5-13. He told the story of someone desperately needing bread from a friend's house because someone visited him at midnight. Although the friend initially refused to help because it was midnight, eventually he agreed. Not because of friendship—they were already friends—but because of persistence (Luke 11:8). He then promised that, *"Everyone who asks receives; the one who seeks finds; and to the one who knocks, the door will be opened"* (Luke 11:10). He then reasoned with them by telling them, *"If you then, though you are evil, know how to give good gifts to your children, how much more will your Father in heaven give the Holy Spirit to those who ask him!"* (Luke 11:13).

To summarize this chapter, every born-again believer has the faith needed to get healed or heal others in the name of Jesus. Jesus never asked us to have *great faith*. In actual fact, when the apostles asked Him to increase their faith, He answered them by saying, *"If you have faith as small as a mustard seed, you can say to this mulberry tree, 'Be uprooted and planted in the sea,' and it will obey you"* (Luke 17:6). Jesus likened the Kingdom of Heaven to a mustard seed planted in a field. While it's the smallest seed, it has all the potential of becoming a large tree, and birds come and make nests in its branches (Matthew

13:32). Jesus was teaching them that it's not the quantity but the quality of the seed. If you have faith through being born again, you have what it takes.

When teaching believers to pray for the sick, James doesn't ask them to have *great faith*, otherwise the healing won't happen. He simply instructs to call for the elders of the church—the mature believers, not according to age, but to spiritual maturity—and pray. Then he says, *"The prayer offered in faith will make the sick person well"* (James 5:15). This verse is simply teaching that mature believers pray in faith, live in faith, move in faith, and heal the sick in faith. This truth is powerful as we believers begin to move in faith and be sure that we have what it takes. We have Jesus, who is our Healer, Savior, and Deliverer. Let's tear down every lie of the enemy that tells us that we don't have "great faith." We have what it takes to walk in the supernatural power of God—because of our union with Christ.

Concluding Prayer

I personally want to thank you for reading this book and hope that you really enjoyed it. I pray it has blessed your life and enlightened your understanding about the subject of divine healing. I pray that the nature of God as healer is set as concrete in your heart and mind. I pray that your level of intimacy with the healer is escalated to the highest level. May you understand your identity in Christ and the incredible greatness of His power to heal, save, and deliver.

May you be His feet and hands in this world to destroy the works of the devil like He did. May you operate in the *full* authority of Christ to heal every sickness and disease.

If you are sick and in need of healing, I invite you to pray this prayer with me:

Dear heavenly Father,

Thank You for paying the full price of my sickness and disease on the cross. Thank You that it is Your will and desire to heal me.

I rebuke all sickness, pain, and disease in the mighty Name of Jesus, and I believe that the Name of Jesus is higher than every other name.

Lord Jesus, I declare that by Your stripes I have been healed. I receive this healing into my spirit, soul, and body right now!

And I speak wholeness and healing to my body in the mighty Name of Jesus.

Amen!

ABOUT YVON ATTIA

Yvon Attia is a radical lover of Jesus and His Word, fully dedicated to His purposes and His call. She shares a very special, deep, and intimate relationship with the Holy Spirit, which people see and feel from the moment they hear her. For those who don't know her name, she has been given the title, "Holy Spirit lady." Yvon finds this to be an honor and great privilege.

She was called into full-time ministry after she powerfully received the baptism of the Holy Spirit at the age of thirty-three and encountered many powerful supernatural instances. Despite the many challenges she faced, Yvon has remained faithful to God and His call. Her mandate, alongside her husband, is to teach and equip ordinary believers to know their identity in Christ and walk in God's supernatural power all the days of their lives.

Yvon is an author and a passionate and powerful speaker who preaches the Word with the power of God's Spirit and the manifestation of His presence. She unpacks the Word from a Middle Eastern perspective, explaining its depth in terms of culture, context, and power.

Yvon has been married to her high-school sweetheart for twenty-two years and they have two beautiful children, Esther and Raphael.

Both Yvon and her husband are ordained pastors under the spiritual fatherhood covering of Apostle Guillermo Maldonado of King Jesus International Ministry in Miami. Miracles of healing take place during their meetings as God faithfully confirms the word through signs that follow.

They are the founders of Celebrate Freedom Ministry, which is part of the supernatural global network of King Jesus International Ministry. Their mandate is to bring God's supernatural power to this generation. They conduct powerful events to teach believers about the healing power of God that is available to every believer. They equip believers to walk in God's supernatural power and impart into them what they have received from God.

Yvon is a qualified teacher who holds a bachelor's degree in education from the University of Sydney. She has completed a master's degree in Christian education from Alphacrucis College in Australia and is currently studying her doctoral studies in ministry. She is currently teaching theology at the University of the Supernatural at King Jesus International Ministry in Miami.

Yvon and her husband Mina broadcast a weekly Christian Arabic program about divine healing on the Middle East's largest Arabic Christian Channel, which reaches millions of people, many of whom are Muslim. Through this program, they have seen God heal thousands of people from all sorts of conditions.

Experience a personal revival!

Spirit-empowered content from today's top Christian authors delivered directly to your inbox.

Join today!
lovetoreadclub.com

Inspiring Articles
Powerful Video Teaching
Resources for Revival

Get all of this and so much more, e-mailed to you twice weekly!

LOVE TO READ CLUB
by **D DESTINY IMAGE**